SO-BDK-287

True and Reasonable

True and Reasonable

In Defense of the Christian Faith

RONALD F. SATTA

WIPF & STOCK · Eugene, Oregon

TRUE AND REASONABLE
In Defense of the Christian Faith

Copyright © 2009 Ronald F. Satta. All rights reserved. Except for brief quotations in critical publications or reviews, no part of this book may be reproduced in any manner without prior written permission from the publisher. Write: Permissions, Wipf and Stock Publishers, 199 W. 8th Ave., Suite 3, Eugene, OR 97401.

Wipf & Stock
A Division of Wipf and Stock Publishers
199 W. 8th Ave., Suite 3
Eugene, OR 97401
www.wipfandstock.com

ISBN 13: 978-1-60608-486-1

Manufactured in the U.S.A.

Unless otherwise stated, Scripture quotations are from the New International Version.

Dedicated to all those on an earnest quest for the truth

Contents

Disclosure ix

Introduction xi

1 THEISM: THE MOST COMPELLING OPTION 1

      The Finite Universe and Its Physical Laws

      The Failure of Naturalism

      The Complexity of the Cell

      Biological Racism: A Case Study of Pseudo Science

2 SCRIPTURE: THE MOST RELIABLE SOURCE 34

      The Orthodox Opinion of the Bible

      Its Internal Testimony

      Historical and Geographical Precision

      Fulfilled Prophecy

3 JESUS THE CHRIST: THE PROMISED MESSIAH 64

      The Historicity of the Crucifixion

      The Likelihood of the Resurrection

      The Coherent Theme of the Bible

      Conclusion

Bibliography 81

Disclosure

I AM THE THANKFUL recipient of the grace of God through Jesus Christ. My experience is one in concert with that of the Apostle Paul who wrote, "Having been justified by faith, we have peace with God through our Lord Jesus Christ" (Rom 5:1). It is my privilege to serve Christ as a preacher of the gospel and a teacher of the Word of God. This calling has occupied much of my professional life for the better part of 30 years. Higher education has filled in the gaps.

Over the course of these years, I have had the good fortune to pursue my passion for intellectual inquiry, earning degrees in communication, New Testament language and literature, preaching, and history, which represents an investment equivalent to 18 years of full-time study in higher education.

During my PhD studies at the University of Rochester, I taught in the reasoning and writing program. Upon completion of my PhD, I taught as an associate faculty member at Brockport College, a member of the State University of New York system. At both institutions, I received awards for excellence in teaching. Additionally, I earned two other academic prizes for doctoral research from the University of Rochester.

I do not think that my faith disqualifies or even hinders me in conducting an analysis of this sort. Indeed, I have always found it bewildering that atheists, many of whom conduct their work with zeal comparable to the most ardent evangelist, are treated as though their prior commitments do not influence their research or conclusions. Everyone, religious or otherwise, has deeply held convictions, concerning which much is at stake—whether it is tenure, grants, reputation, or something else. It seems to me that the best we can do is confront our bias honestly and work hard to treat the evidence fairly in spite of it—wherever it leads. This is hard to do—for everyone.

This book is intended to be analytical, informative, and persuasive. Be forewarned, I am a committed evangelical who believes theism is intellectually superior to atheism. Furthermore, I contend that the Christian faith is endorsed by considerable philosophical, scientific, historical, and biblical evidence, making its truth claims highly probable. As the Apostle Paul endeavored to reason with and persuade his ancient audience of the truth of his message, so I will do precisely the same thing for my modern audience. Of course, the reader will judge the degree to which this mission is accomplished.

For the Truth,

RFS

Introduction

I N THE BIBLE, FAITH is contrasted with sight, not with reason. Paul, the apostle, consistently reasoned with his listeners, persuading them regarding the truth of his message, establishing a precedent for Christian apologetics (Acts 17:17; 18:4; and 18:19). He did so because the Christian faith is reasonable.

This apologetic begins with arguments in favor of theism: the finite universe and its physical laws that are hospitable to life, the origin and complexity of life, and the failure of naturalism as explanator. These factors suggest the existence of a brilliant and powerful Creator who designed the universe, our world, and us. Such a conclusion is in harmony with rational deduction. To assert otherwise requires an enormous amount of faith in chance, lacking sufficient warrant and contrary to logical inference.

But is it possible to know the designer? I believe that it is. The next chapter deals with the authority of Scripture and more precisely with why the Bible is superior to every other source, legitimizing its claim to divine origin. Biblical inerrancy represents essential orthodoxy both because of Scripture's commentary to that effect and its exacting accuracy in matters that can be tested. For instance, the geographical and historical reliability of Scripture is in accord with a high view of inspiration. This alone does not prove the Bible's divine origin, but it does elevate its status as a conveyor of accurate, reliable information.

Furthermore, Bible prophecy, in which the text predicts future events with startling precision, will be examined. This predictive element makes Scripture unique. While liberal theologians attempt to dismiss this through dating techniques that turn prophecy into history, such tactics are futile against many prophecies. This is especially true regarding those that speak to and about Christ.

Several key prophetic passages will be considered including Isaiah 53 and Daniel 9. Since it is humanly impossible to accurately forecast the future with specificity, the fact that Scripture consistently does so indicates that it is a special composition whose message about the designer should be carefully considered.

Chapter three turns from the authority of the Bible to the person of Jesus Christ. He alone fulfills the prophecies of Isaiah, Daniel, and the other prophets. The crucifixion of Jesus, of which the seers wrote, is the best-attested event in antiquity. Indeed, if we reliably know anything about the distant past, we know that Jesus was crucified by Pontius Pilate. This is verified by sympathetic and unsympathetic witnesses.

Moreover, the cohesive message of the apostles—the primary sources—following the execution of Jesus, even under considerable duress, further testifies to the reality of the bodily resurrection of Christ. When these factors are combined, the Christian faith is endorsed by considerable philosophical, scientific, historical, and biblical evidence, making its truth claims quite probable, intellectually satisfying, and entirely reasonable.

Theism: The Most Compelling Option

*You are worthy, our Lord and God, to receive glory and honor
and power, for you created all things, and by your will
they were created and have their being.*

Revelation 4:11

"ELEMENTARY, MY DEAR WATSON." These familiar words of deductive triumph belong to the fictional super sleuth Sherlock Holmes. But one need not be an investigative genius in order to effectively exercise rational deduction and logical inference through observation. We do it all the time.

Many disciplines could not function without doing so. An archaeologist uncovers primitive pottery at a dig and concludes that someone made it. No one considers that rash even though the individuals responsible have long since disappeared. A historian examines a Civil War battlefield, discovering a number of relics including some bullets and a battered musket in the process. He never questions that the bullets were fired and that the weapon was designed.

Lawyers consult on a criminal court case, discovering that there are no eye witnesses. They do not wring their hands but get busy examining circumstantial evidence. Piece by piece the attorneys reconstruct the scene of the crime and more often than not solve the case beyond a reasonable doubt. Moreover, most people feel entirely satisfied with such closure—all except the convicted person perhaps.

If I walk into my office area, as I did recently, and smell popcorn, it is completely legitimate to assume someone had recently popped it. Though no one was visible, I knew they had been there. The aroma gave them away. All of this is axiomatic, self-evident, intuitive. Yet some people still assert that it is impossible to detect the presence of God because one cannot see God. This is bogus. The circumstantial evidence gives him away.

Deduction and inference through observation are reliable methods of detecting presence whether or not the primary agent is accessible. In this chapter, I argue that theism is a far more compelling option than atheism. The argument unfolds along several lines: the finite universe and its physical laws, the amazing complexity of life, and the failure of naturalism to account for it. In each case, through the use of rational deduction and logical inference, the presence of a Creator is detectable.

THE FINITE UNIVERSE AND ITS PHYSICAL LAWS

Whatever begins to exist has a cause. The universe began to exist.
Therefore, the universe has a cause.

The Kalam Cosmological Argument

Today, it is generally agreed upon by scientists in the fields of astronomy and astrophysics that the universe in fact had a beginning.[1] At one time, many considered the universe to be infinite, eternal, a self-directed and sustaining entity with no nascent point. Theists, who disagreed, were left to argue philosophically that actual infinity was impossible in real time and space. Thus the universe, they urged, must have begun. One of their most compelling arguments revolved around the idea that infinity could never be attained by means of addition, because in addition another element can always be introduced to the equation regardless of its amount.[2]

Since the chronological movement of time is calculated sequentially, one moment following the next, that movement is in essence by addition. Theists reasoned that since a chronological sequence of movements by addition could never achieve infinity and that time is such a move-

---

1. Craig, *Kalam Cosmological Argument*, 110. I am indebted to the cogent argument provided by William Lane Craig regarding both the philosophical and scientific arguments favoring a finite universe. Philosophically, Craig argues that an actually infinite regress is impossible to achieve in real time and space. Particularly is this true when dealing with the sequential movement of time via addition—one moment following the next, since infinity can never be reached by means of addition—one can always add another element to the equation. He appeals to evidence regarding the expanding universe and thermodynamics to establish the case scientifically—and to my mind it is a compelling one, indeed. For a condensed version of Craig's comments see Strobel, *Case for a Creator*, 93–123.

2. See especially Craig, *Kalam Argument*, 102–5.

ment, then the universe of actual time and space could not be eternal. Of course, they also appealed to their faith in God as the creating agent of the universe in harmony with their sacred traditions. But, that was not a legitimate argument to their detractors.

Science has recently aligned with philosophy to buttress the contention that the universe began. This conclusion is partially the result of the work of Edwin Hubble who discovered in 1929 that the universe is actually expanding—and expanding "isotropically" or in all directions at once. William Lane Craig comments on this discovery:

> The staggering implication of this (expansion) is that by thus extrapolating back into the past, we come to a point in time at which *the entire known universe was contracted into an arbitrarily great density*; if one extrapolates the motion of the galaxies into the past as far as possible, one reaches a state of contraction of infinite density. If the velocity of the galaxies has remained unchanged . . . the universe began to expand from a state of *infinite density* in what has come to be called the "big bang."[3]

Amazing! Our universe began from an infinitesimally small point of immense density. Some scientists find this disturbing, even irksome. I suspect the reason for their angst is related to the metaphysical and theological implications attending this fact. It is here that the Kalam argument is particularly incisive. It states,

> Whatever begins to exist has a cause. The universe began to exist. Therefore, the universe has a cause.

It is the causal element that is at the root of concern for many materialists. So long as the universe was considered infinite, one could attribute its existence to natural forces, those forces inherently present in the physical realm. Such a universe did not require an explanation; it just was. Reality was hermetically sealed within the confines of the physical world. Generally, naturalists prefer such a model because it supports their philosophical bias that the natural world is all there is and that natural laws or forces can explain everything.

But the logic of the Kalam argument is sound. The first premise, "Whatever begins to exist has a cause," is largely self-evident, harmonizing with all our experience and knowledge. The second premise, "The universe began to exist," is now verified by science. Thus, the third prem-

3. Ibid., 113.

ise, "Therefore, the universe has a cause," follows cogently. Hence, we are confronted with a finite universe that owes its existence to some causal agent. So either the universe was caused by something or by nothing. But the second option is absurd since everyone knows that nothing cannot create everything—in fact, nothing can't create anything. So something is a better option—but what was the causal agent?[4]

I suggest that based upon the product of the universe itself—the consequence of the bang, its scope, and the physical laws operative within it—some legitimate deductions and inferences are possible. First, let us remind ourselves that most explosions are destructive, particularly those of great magnitude. Surely one would be hard pressed to imagine an explosion of greater force than the one currently under discussion. Yet the consequence of this immense eruption did not result in carnage. The end product was a universe not in ruins but one ready for and hospitable to human life. As a matter of fact, the physical laws that prevail in our universe appear meticulously programmed in favor of life.

Over the course of the last 30 years or so, the "anthropic principle" has become an increasingly powerful argument for design. Cambridge physicist Brandon Carter first used the phrase in 1973 to describe the singular unifying feature found among the various laws of physics which

4. The necessary implication of the Big Bang Theory is that the universe began out of nothing—or ex nihilo. Some scientists refuse to accept this, appealing to other models like the Steady-State or the oscillating universe model. But advances in physics have made both appear unlikely. Stanley Jaki states, "As a matter of fact, the theory (Steady-State model) has failed so far to secure a single piece of experimental verification [parenthesis mine]. In addition to this and the preposterous concept of spontaneous creation (creation out of nothing with no causal agent), together with its overtly anti-theological, or rather anti-Christian, motivations it should be pointed out about the Steady-State Theory that it is but a subclass of cosmologies based upon the ideas of perpetual returns [parenthesis mine]. 'The . . . principle on which the Steady-State Theory is based, would in itself allow both the expansion and contraction of the universe, but the latter possibility is rejected for the reason that in such a case there would be even more radiation compared with matter than in a static universe.' The expansion is accepted out of deference for the observational evidence and also because a basically static universe would have long reached an equilibrium state." And in opposition to the oscillating theory Jaki quotes from H. Dingle's presidential address to the Royal Astronomical Society, "Every process we know, on the small or the large scale, is a one-way process, showing a preference for one direction over the opposite. The system of nebulae expands and does not contract, gravitation is an attraction and not a repulsion, the entropy of a closed system increases and does not decrease, every chemical process tends towards a state of equilibrium from which the substances concerned do not of themselves depart. . . . There is nothing whatever in nature that indicates that any course of events is reversible." Jaki, *Science and Creation,* 347–48.

seem to converge around the purpose of promoting and maintaining life. In other words, the laws of nuclear physics seem to suggest that the universe was expecting us.[5]

5. Though the authors of the *Anthropic Cosmological Principle* are opposed to using it in support of design, they nonetheless concede, "Thus the modern anthropic principles can be seen partly as natural consequences of the fact that current physical theories are extremely successful. This success is still a mystery. . . . It is also, in part, a consequence of the fact that we have found nature to be constructed upon certain immutable foundation stones, which we call fundamental constants of nature. As yet, we have no explanation for the precise numerical values taken by these unchanging dimensionless numbers. They are not subject to evolution or selection by any known natural or unnatural mechanism. The fortuitous nature of many of their numerical values is a mystery that cries out for solution." Barrow and Tipler, *Anthropic Cosmological Principle,* 31.

Other scientists believe that this mystery defies any natural solution, arguing that such meticulous settings require an intelligent source, "For instance, let's talk about gravity. . . . Imagine a ruler, or one of those old-fashioned linear radio dials, that goes all the way across the universe. It would be broken down into one-inch increments, which means there would be billions upon billions upon billions of inches. The entire dial represents the range of force strengths in nature, with gravity being the weakest force and the strong force that binds protons and neutrons together in the nuclei being the strongest, a whopping ten thousand billion, billion, billion, billion, times stronger than gravity. The range of possible settings for the force of gravity can plausibly be taken to be at least as large as the total range of force strengths. Now let's imagine that you want to move the dial from where it's currently set. Even if you were to move it by only one inch, the impact on life in the universe would be catastrophic. . . . Of all the possible settings on the dial, from one side of the universe to the other, it happens to be situated in the exact right fraction of an inch to make our universe capable of sustaining life." Collins, "Evidence of Physics," 131–32. Bill Bryson underscores the amazing precision of these physical calibrations when he notes, "For the universe to exist as it does requires that hydrogen be converted to helium in a precise . . . manner—specifically, in a way that converts seven one thousandths of its mass to energy. Lower that value very slightly—from 0.007 percent to 0.006 percent, say—and no transformation could take place: the universe would consist of hydrogen and nothing else. Raise the value very slightly—to 0.008 percent—and bonding would be so wildly prolific that the hydrogen would long since have been exhausted. In either case, with the slightest tweaking of the numbers the universe as we know and need it would not be here." Bryson, *Short History of Nearly Everything,* 24–25.

Bryson further states, "According to Guth's theory, at one ten-millionth of a trillionth of a trillionth of a trillionth of a second, gravity emerged. After another ludicrously brief interval it was joined by electromagnetism and the strong and weak nuclear forces—the stuff of physics. These were joined an instant later by swarms of elementary particles—the stuff of stuff. From nothing at all, suddenly there were swarms of photons, protons, electrons, neutrons, and much else . . . in a single crackling instant we were endowed with a universe that was vast—at least a hundred billion light years across. . . . What is extraordinary from our point of view is how well it turned out for us. If the universe had formed just a tiny bit differently—if gravity were fractionally stronger or weaker, if the expansion had proceeded just a little more slowly or swiftly—then there might never have been stable elements to make you and me and the ground we stand on. Had gravity been a

Factors such as the rate at which stars produce oxygen and carbon, the ratio by which hydrogen converts to helium, the constant energy density of empty space, and the degree of gravitational force, all intersect to promote, protect, and preserve life. The odds of such harmony occurring randomly as a consequence of an explosion are staggering. As a matter of fact, believing that even one such law would spontaneously and randomly turn in our favor requires an enormous amount of faith in chance—nearly beyond imagination. Out of the billions of potential settings, all the physical laws are calibrated with exacting precision to optimal life-benefiting positions.

Perhaps this is why the acclaimed astrophysicist Sir Fred Hoyle commented, "I do not believe that any scientists who examined the evidence would fail to draw the logical inference that the laws of nuclear physics have been deliberately designed with regard to the consequences they produce inside stars. If this is so, then my apparently random quirks have become part of a deep laid scheme. If not, then we are back again at a monstrous sequence of accidents."[6] It is not likely that Hoyle transgressed

---

trifle stronger, the universe itself might have collapsed like a badly erected tent, without precisely the right values to give it the right dimensions and density and component parts. Had it been weaker, however, nothing would have coalesced. The universe would have remained forever a dull, scattered void." Ibid., 22–23.

Some estimates suggest that there are as many as thirty such parameters, each needing the same sort of pinpoint adjustment in order to produce a universe suitable for life. Stephen Meyer states, "Explaining anthropic coincidences as the product of chance . . . has several severe liabilities. . . . First, the immense improbability of the fine tuning makes straightforward appeals to chance untenable. Physicists have discovered more than thirty separate physical or cosmological parameters that require precise calibration in order to produce a life-sustaining universe. Michael Denton, in his book *Nature's Destiny* (1998), has documented many other necessary conditions for specifically human life from chemistry, geology, and biology. Moreover, many individual parameters exhibit an extraordinarily high degree of fine tuning. . . . In many cases, the odds of arriving at a single correct setting by chance, let alone all the correct settings, turn out to be virtually infinitesimal. Oxford physicist Roger Penrose has noted that a single parameter, the so-called 'original phase-space volume,' required such precise fine tuning that the 'Creator's aim must have been [precise] to an accuracy of one part in . . . ten billion multiplied by itself 123 times.' Penrose goes on to remark that 'one could not possibly even write the number down in full . . . [since] it would be "1" followed by 1023 successive "0"s!'—more zeroes than the number of elementary particles in the entire universe. Such is, he concludes, 'the precision needed to set the universe on its course.'" Meyer, *Science and Evidence for Design*, 60–61. To suppose that these settings all randomly landed in exactly the right place unassisted and by chance seems quite simply beyond all reason. Indeed, to feel satisfied with such a conviction requires an enormous amount of unwarranted faith.

6. Barrow and Tipler, *Anthropic Cosmological Principle*, 22.

the bounds of reason in his assessment, especially in light of similar comments made by other eminent scientists. For instance, Owen Gingerich, Harvard astronomy professor, concurred with Hoyle's judgment noting, "Fred Hoyle and I differ on lots of questions, but on this we agree: a common sense and satisfying interpretation of our world suggests the designing hand of a superintelligence."[7]

Not surprisingly, Darwinians chafe against such concessions, but at the most fundamental level their resistance amounts to non-sequitur. They believe that the physical world represents reality—in total—entirely.[8] There is nothing else and nothing more. However, this fundamental point to their philosophical worldview is flawed. Since the universe began, and whatever begins to exist has a cause, the universe is the product of a causal agent who transcends the natural world. To assert that the universe self-

---

7. Gingerich, "Dare a Scientist Believe?" 25. "Despite the articulate denials of cosmic teleology by the leading evolutionists of our age, there still remain enough astonishing details of the natural order to evoke a feeling of awe—so much so that cosmologists have even given it a name: the anthropic principle." Gingerich goes on to state, "I am told that Fred Hoyle, who together with Willy Fowler found this remarkable nuclear arrangement, has said that nothing has shaken his atheism as much as this discovery. Occasionally Fred Hoyle and I have sat down to discuss one or another astronomical or historical point, but I never had enough nerve to ask him if his atheism had really been shaken by finding the nuclear resonance structure of carbon and oxygen. However, the answer came rather clearly in the November 1981 issue of the Cal Tech alumni magazine, where he wrote: 'A common sense interpretation of the facts suggests that a superintellect has monkeyed with the physics, as well as with chemistry and biology, and that there are no blind forces worth speaking about in nature. The numbers one calculates from the facts seem to me so overwhelming as to put this conclusion almost beyond question.'. . . Impressive as the evidences of design in the astrophysical world may be, however, I personally find even more remarkable those from the biological realm. . . . Even Hoyle, by his allusion to . . . biology, seems to agree that the formation, say of DNA, is so improbable as to require a superintelligence. Such biochemical arguments were popularized about forty years ago by Lecompte du Nouy in his book *Human Destiny*. Du Nouy estimated the probability of forming a two-thousand-atom protein as something like one part in 10^{321}. 'Events which, even when we admit very numerous experiments, reactions, or shakings per second, *need an infinitely longer time than the estimated duration of the earth in order to have one chance, on the average, to manifest themselves can, it would seem, be considered as impossible in the human sense.*'" Gingerich, "Dare a Scientist Believe?" 23–26.

8. "Since the singularity occurs at a finite time in the past, there is a temptation to ask the question, 'What happened before the singularity?' However, this question makes as much sense as the question, 'What happened before the universe began, assuming it has existed forever?' Nothing happened before, because there is no before in either case." Barrow and Tipler, *Anthropic Cosmological Principle*, 442. But something did, in fact, precede the moment of the explosion.

generated spontaneously is patently ridiculous. Something other than the universe is responsible for it—something beyond it. By necessity it was something different, something supra-natural. Thus at the level of first principles, naturalism is already defeated.

What might one reasonably conclude about the causal agent based upon the product conceived? First, it seems reasonable to conclude that the cause is powerful, very powerful, frighteningly powerful. Second, that the cause is brilliant, vastly brilliant beyond anything we can imagine. Third, it would appear the cause is benevolent, having taken great pains to create a hospitable environment in which human life can flourish.

THE FAILURE OF NATURALISM

*If evolution means the gradual change of one kind of organism
into another, the outstanding characteristic of the fossil record
is the absence of evidence for evolution.*

Phillip Johnson, legal scholar

Darwinian naturalism contends that all life is attributable to descent through modification governed by natural selection. All species evolved from a single simple cell organism and thus all share a common ancestry. Evolution theory is taught as a fact in public school systems throughout America and has thus become the politically acceptable answer to the question of origins. But from its inception, critics have maintained that the idea was dignified with intellectual respectability mostly for philosophical rather than empirical reasons. While most of its early detractors were geologists (for reasons which shall become apparent presently), theologian Charles Hodge, a contemporary of Darwin, showed keen insight when he observed:

> When the theory of evolution was propounded in 1844 in the "Vestiges of Creation," it was universally rejected; when proposed by Mr. Darwin, less than twenty years afterward, it was received with acclamation. Why is this? The facts are now what they were then . . . How then is it, that what was scientifically false in 1844 is scientifically true in 1864? . . . There is only one cause for the fact referred to, that we can think of. The "Vestiges of Creation"; did not expressly or effectually exclude design. Darwin does. This is

a reason assigned by the most zealous advocates of his theory for their adoption of it.[9]

In other words, Hodge argued that Darwin gained favor because he denied design in the created order, appealing instead to chance natural consequences as the sole mechanism of creative activity. For instance, Darwin asserted that the organ of the eye developed randomly with no prior plan to produce an instrument of sight. Everything was a product of chance not design—the cardio-vascular system, the visual system, the auditory system, the nervous system, the digestive system, the reproductive system—everything originated by chance.

This idea offered adherents liberation from divine accountability. It pleased the social sensibilities of the time and was thus adopted as a legitimate possibility even though the experimental verification was paltry. I submit that what was true then is equally true today. Darwinism is maintained because it serves an important social function, buttressing the dominant intellectual philosophy of materialism.

9. C. Hodge, *What is Darwinism?* 145–6. Hodge observed that Darwin had credited Lamarck with suggesting, as early as 1811, that all species had descended from other species. He also asserted that the concept of natural selection appeared in earlier works as well, especially in "The Vestiges of Creation" produced in 1844. The truly unique element of Darwinian evolution was its obvious exclusion of a Designer. Hodge stated in this regard, "It is however neither evolution nor natural selection which give Darwinism its peculiar character and importance. It is that Darwin rejects all teleology, or the doctrine of final causes. He denies design in any of the organisms in the vegetable or animal world. He teaches that the eye was formed without any purpose of producing an organ of vision." Ibid., 48–52. Hodge marshaled an impressive defense against Darwinism, most particularly considering the limited nature of the sciences at his disposal. He noted, "that the fixedness of species made macroevolution appear quite untenable. Since hybrids possessed no ability to procreate, it appeared that 'God has fixed limits which cannot be passed.' Even such a naturalist as Thomas Huxley admitted that this represented an 'insuperable objection' to Darwinian gradualism.... Particularly troubling to Darwin and fascinating to Hodge were cases of insect neuters—the sterile females within an insect community. Darwin noted that these insects often differed widely in both their instincts and anatomic structures from male and fertile females. The problem for gradualism, of course, was that they could not propagate themselves, meaning that natural selection failed as an explanatory mechanism for their development. Furthermore, Hodge observed, these neuters were not degenerations, but were frequently 'larger and more robust than their associates.' Obviously, it is difficult to imagine how natural selection could be credited with such infertile consequences, since these insects did not reproduce and sterility could not be considered advantageous to the survivability of the neuters under any quantifiably reasonable measure." Satta, *Sacred Text*, 50–51.

Many volumes, scores and scores of volumes, have been written about Darwinian naturalism—for and against. Let me briefly set forth what I consider insuperable problems associated with naturalism as an explanatory mechanism. Of course, I do not suspect that ardent devotees of materialism will feel the same way—they have far too much at stake. Fortunately, I am writing to those of a candid mind. I am confident that by observation and inference, design prevails as the most compelling model.

I suspect most people believe that the fossil record is a strong ally of Darwinism. It isn't. As a matter of fact, it has become an embarrassing liability. Darwin believed that in time the transitional forms, which *must have existed* if his theory is sound, would be discovered. He noted in this regard, "why, if species have descended from other species by insensibly fine gradations, do we not everywhere see innumerable transitional forms?"[10] Why, indeed! Time has not been kind to Darwinians. After 150 years of dedicated—even desperate—digging, the missing links are still missing and missing en masse. Darwin expected thousands of such intermediates to materialize through excavation. He was quite right to expect this.[11]

---

10. Darwin, *Origin of Species*, 205. Darwin realized that such glaring omissions, if remained unchecked, had the power to condemn his idea. He wrote, "The number of intermediate varieties which have formerly existed on the earth must be enormous. Why then is not every geological formation and every stratum full of such intermediate links? Geology assuredly does not reveal any such finely graduated organic chain; and this is perhaps the most obvious and gravest objection which can be urged against my theory." And again he puzzled, "But, by this theory innumerable transitional forms must have existed, why do we not find them embedded in countless numbers in the crust of the earth?" He candidly admitted, "The several difficulties here discussed, namely our not finding in the successive formations infinitely numerous transitional links between the many species which now exist or have existed; the sudden manner in which whole groups of species appear ... the almost entire absence ... of fossiliferous formations beneath the Silurian strata, are all undoubtedly of the gravest nature." Ibid., 287, 206, and 315.

11. Indeed Darwinian naturalism is utterly dependent upon slight modification in organisms over vast sums of time to work its "magic." Richard Dawkins asserts, "No matter how improbable it is that an X could have arisen from a Y in a single step, it is always possible to conceive of a series of infinitesimally graded intermediates in between them. However improbable a large-scale change may be, smaller changes are less improbable. And provided we postulate a sufficiently large series of sufficiently finely graded intermediates, we shall be able to derive anything from anything else, without invoking astronomical probabilities. We are allowed to do this only if there has been sufficient time to fit all the intermediaries in." Dawkins, *Blind Watchmaker*, 317–8. Of course, the inquisitive mind is left asking where then is the evidence for these finely graded intermediary forms?

Indeed, the hypothesis submitted by Dawkins stands decidedly out of concert with

Just think about it. In regard to mammals, we find such marvelously discrete groups as bats, whales, bears, kangaroos, monkeys, cattle, cats, pigs, etc. For each group, innumerable transitional forms must exist. But the silence of the fossil evidence is deafening. Darwinists seek to mitigate the effects of such omissions, by arguing either that the transitional forms may yet be found or that they somehow escaped fossilization. But no matter how adept Darwinists are at evading the issue, one point must be stressed, namely, that they are forced to defend their position *from* the evidence instead of supporting it *by* the evidence. Naturalists are relegated to maintaining their theory *in spite of the facts* not because of them.[12] But the evidence from the fossil record only gets worse for gradualism.

the evidence of the case, as Michael Denton points out, "The overall character of the fossil record as it stands today was superbly summarized in an article by G.G. Simpson prepared for the Darwin Centenary Symposium held in Chicago in 1959. Simpson is a leading paleontologist whose testimony to the reality of the gaps in the fossil record has considerable force. As he points out, it is one of the most striking features of the fossil record that most new kinds of organisms appear abruptly: 'They are not, as a rule, led up to by a sequence of almost imperceptibly changing forerunners such as Darwin believed should be usual in evolution. A great many sequences of two or a few temporally intergrading species are known, but even at this level most species appear without known immediate ancestors. . . .' In effect Simpson is admitting that the fossils provide none of the crucial transitional forms required by evolution. . . . The virtual complete absence of intermediate and ancestral forms from the fossil record is today recognized widely by many leading paleontologists as one of its most striking characteristics, so much so that those authorities . . . now take it as axiomatic, that, in attempting to determine the relationships of fossil species, in the words of a recent British Museum publication: 'we assume that none of the fossil species we are considering is the ancestor of the other.' " Denton, *Evolution*, 164–65.

12. Denton observes further, "while the rocks have continually yielded new and exciting and even bizarre forms of life . . . what they have never yielded is any of Darwin's myriads of transitional forms. Despite the tremendous increase in geological activity in every corner of the globe and despite the discovery of many strange and hitherto unknown forms, the infinitude of connecting links has still not been discovered and the fossil record is about as discontinuous as it was when Darwin was writing *Origin*. The intermediates have remained as elusive as ever and their absence remains, a century later, one of the most striking characteristics of the fossil record. It is still, as it was in Darwin's day, overwhelmingly true that the first representatives of all the major classes of organisms known to biology are already highly characteristic of their class when they make their initial appearance in the fossil record. . . . At its first appearance in the ancient Paleozoic seas, invertebrate life was already divided into practically all the major groups with which we are familiar today. . . . The same pattern is true of the vertebrate fossil record. The first members of each major group appear abruptly, unlinked to other groups by transitional or intermediate forms. Already at their first appearance . . . they are well differentiated and already characteristic of their respective classes. Take, for example, the

If Darwin were right, one would expect that primitive forms of life would exhibit relative simplicity and gradually across time become increasingly complex and divergent through descent with modification guided by natural selection. Such a prediction attributes an enormous amount of creative energy to natural selection—a creativity that far eclipses minor variation within a species. Instead, the fantastic power to create macro-variation is invoked for selection, producing entirely new organs, skeletal structures, external casings, and in short entirely new species. Variation within species diminishes genetic information but macroevolution would demand a huge surge in genetic technology.[13] However, no evidence exists indicating that natural selection wields such awesome prowess.

Many prominent evolutionists agree that the fossil record does not support gradualism. Perhaps best known among them is the Harvard scientist Stephen Jay Gould, now deceased. Gould noted:

---

way the various fish groups make their appearance.... The first representatives of all these groups were already so highly differentiated and isolated at their first appearance that none of them can be considered even in the remotest sense as intermediate with regard to other groups. The story is the same for ... sharks and rays.... At their first appearance they too are highly specialized and quite distinct and isolated from the earlier fish groups. No fish group known to vertebrate paleontology can be classed as an ancestor of another; all are related as sister groups, never as ancestors and descendants." Ibid., 162–4.

13. As Davis and Kenyon note, "Macroevolution requires an increase of the gene pool, the addition of new genetic information, whereas the means to speciation ... represent the loss of genetic information. Both physical and ecological isolation produce varieties by cutting a small population off from its parent population. A large population carries a genetic reserve, a wealth of concealed recessive genes. In a small group cut off from the parent population, some of these recessive traits may be expressed more often. This makes for interesting diversity, but it should not blind us to the fact that the total genetic variability in the small group is reduced. The appearance of reproductively isolated populations represents microevolution not macroevolution. It is one of the ways in which horizontal diversification can occur.... Vertical change—to new levels of complexity—requires the input of additional genetic information. Can that information—the ensembles of new genes to make wrens, rabbits, and hawthorne trees be gleaned from random mutations? Thus far, there appears to be good evidence that the roles mutations are able to play are severely restricted by and within the existing higher level blueprint of the organism's whole genome.... Mechanisms for the loss of genetic information cannot be used as support for a theory requiring vast increases in genetic information. Speciation is actually akin to what breeders do. They isolate a small group of plants or animals and force them to interbreed, cutting them off from the larger gene pool to which they belong. Centuries of breeding testifies to the fact that this produces limited change only. It does not produce the open-ended change required by Darwinian evolution." Davis and Kenyon, *Of Pandas and People*, 19–20.

The history of most fossil species includes two features particularly inconsistent with gradualism: 1) Stasis. Most species exhibit no directional change during their tenure on earth. They appear in the fossil record pretty much the same as when they disappear; morphological change is usually limited and directionless.

2) Sudden appearance. In any local area, a species does not arise gradually by the steady transformation of its ancestors; it appears all at once and fully-formed.[14]

Gould concluded that species typically show up complex and fully formed right from the beginning. Neither do they exhibit significant morphological or structural change across time. Moreover, they tend to show up suddenly, independent of any precursor ancestor. Phillip Johnson, the legal scholar, aptly observed in light of this admission that, "If evolution means the gradual change of one kind of organism into another, the outstanding characteristic of the fossil record is the absence of evidence for evolution."[15]

14. Gould, *Wonderful Life*, quoted in P. Johnson, *Darwin on Trial*, 50. Gould further notes regarding the Cambrian explosion, "This chronology poses the two classic puzzles of the Cambrian explosion—enigmas that obsessed Darwin (1859, pp. 306–10) and remain central riddles of life's history: (1) Why did multi-cellular life appear so late? (2) And why do these anatomically complex creatures have no direct, simpler precursors in the fossil record of Precambrian times? . . . This apparent absence of life during most of the earth's history, and its subsequent appearance at full complexity, posed no problems for anti-evolutionists. Roderick Impey Murchison, the great geologist who first worked out the record of early life, simply viewed the Cambrian explosion as God's moment of creation, and read the complexity of the first animals as a sign that God had invested appropriate care in his initial models . . . Darwin . . . placed the Cambrian explosion at the pinnacle of his distress, and devoted an entire section to this subject in the *Origin of Species*. Darwin acknowledged the anti-evolutionary interpretation of many important geologists: 'Several of the most eminent geologists, with Sir R. Murchison at their head, are convinced that we see in the organic remains of the lowest Silurian stratum (now called Cambrian) the dawn of life on this planet.' . . . Darwin invoked his standard argument to resolve this uncomfortable problem: the fossil record is so imperfect that we do not have evidence for most events of life's history. But even Darwin acknowledged that his favorite ploy was wearing a bit thin . . . the problem of the Cambrian explosion has remained as stubborn as ever—if not more so, since our confusion now rests on knowledge, rather than ignorance, about the nature of Precambrian life." Gould, *Wonderful Life*, 56–57.

15. P. Johnson, *Darwin on Trial*, 50. For those wishing to read more widely on the distress of Darwinism, I recommend this well-reasoned book. Johnson notes, "Darwin acknowledged that his theory implied that 'the number of intermediate and transitional links, between all living and extinct species, must have been inconceivably great.' One might therefore suppose that geologists would be continually uncovering fossil evidence of transitional forms. This, however, was clearly not the case. What geologists did dis-

Nowhere is this abrupt appearance more vivid, startling, and disturbing for Darwinians than in the Cambrian explosion, popularized by Gould's book *Wonderful Life*. Here encased in rock, allegedly 600 million

cover was species, and groups of species, which appeared suddenly rather than at the end of a chain of evolutionary links. Darwin conceded that the state of the fossil evidence was 'the most obvious and gravest objection which can be urged against my theory,' and that it accounted for the fact that 'all the most eminent paleontologists . . . and all our greatest geologists . . . have unanimously, often vehemently, maintained the immutability of species.' . . . Darwin did as well with the fossil problem as the discouraging facts allowed, but to some questions he had to respond frankly that 'I can give no satisfactory answer,' and there is a hint of desperation in his writing at times, as in the following sentence: 'Nature may almost be said to have guarded against the frequent discovery of her transitional or linking forms.'. . . At this point I ask the reader to stop with me for a moment and consider what an unbiased person ought to have thought about the controversy over evolution in the period immediately following the publication of *The Origin of Species*. Opposition to Darwin's theory could hardly be attributed to religious prejudice when the skeptics included the leading paleontologists and geologists of the day. Darwin's defense of the theory of the fossil evidence was not unreasonable, but the point is, it was a *defense*. Very possibly the fossil beds are mere snapshots of moments in geological time, with sufficient time and space between them for a lot of evolution to be going on in the gaps. Still, it is one thing to say that there are gaps, and quite another thing to claim the right to fill the gaps with the evidence required to support one's theory. Darwin's arguments could establish at most that the fossil problem was not fatal; they could not turn the absence of confirming evidence into an asset. There was a way to test the theory by fossil evidence, however, if Darwin and his followers had wanted a test. Darwin was emphatic that the number of transitional intermediaries must have been immense, even 'inconceivable.' Perhaps evidence of their existence was missing because in 1859 only a small part of the world's fossil beds had been searched, and because the explorers had not known what to look for. Once paleontologists accepted Darwinism as a working hypothesis, however, and explored many new fossil beds in an effort to confirm the theory, the situation ought to change. In time the fossil record could be expected to look very different, and very much more Darwinian. The test would not be fair to the skeptics, however, unless it was also possible for the theory to fail. . . . Suppose that paleontologists became so committed to the new way of thinking that fossil studies were published only if they supported the theory, and were discarded as failures if they showed an absence of evolutionary change. As we shall see, that is what happened. Darwinism apparently passed the fossil test, but only because it was not allowed to fail." Ibid., 46–48. Darwinian hopes for a robust emergence of transitional forms have been entirely defeated, as they remain as elusive as they were in Darwin's time. In discussing the Cambrian explosion, Johnson states, "The general picture of animal history is thus a burst of general body plans followed by extinction. No new phyla evolved thereafter . . . we see the basic body plans all appearing first, many of these becoming extinct, and further diversification proceeding strictly within the boundaries of the original phyla. These original Cambrian groups have no visible evolutionary history . . . just about all we have between complex multicellular animals and single cells is some words like 'fast transition.' We can call this thoroughly un-Darwinian scenario 'evolution,' but we are just attaching a label to a mystery." Ibid., 55–56. Johnson's book is clear, cogent, and, to my mind, compelling.

years old, one finds nearly all the animal phyla, without a single trace of ancestral predecessors. These are complex, fully-formed and developed phyla without even the remotest sign of a developmental trail. Without any evolutionary history whatsoever, these sophisticated life forms simply appear as though out of nothing.[16]

Nor is it only animal life which appears inexplicable in gradualistic terms; the same holds for the supposed evolution of plants. The comments of Cambridge botanist E. J. H. Corner are telling: "Can you imagine how an orchid, a duckweed, and a palm have come from the same ancestry, and have we any evidence for this assumption? The evolutionist must be prepared with an answer, but I think that most would break down before an inquisition."[17]

To my mind, the combined force of the fossil evidence effectively refutes Darwinian gradualism. Moreover, one might reasonably contend that the fossil record is the lone piece of concrete historical evidence we possess in an assessment of the distant past. Darwinism is the modern-day equivalent to the story of the king's new clothes. Many people praise it, but its substance is scanty.

Darwinists frequently complain that advocates of special creation offer no positive evidence for their theory but only fault find concerning evolution. But such pouting is as ineffectual as it is inaccurate. Every complaint registered against gradualism is in fact a positive argument in favor of design—for immediacy. For instance, regarding the Cambrian explosion,

16. As Denton further notes, "Curiously, the problem is compounded (the lack of evolutionary ancestors) by the fact that the earliest representatives of most of the major invertebrate phyla appear in the fossil record over a relatively short space of geological time . . . in the Cambrian era. The strata lain down . . . before the Cambrian era, which might have contained the connecting links between the major phyla, are almost completely empty of animal fossils. If transitional types between the major phyla ever existed then it is in these precambrian strata that their fossils should be found." Denton, *Evolution*, 163.

17. Corner, "Evolution," 97. Corner candidly admits that the evidence of plants favors design, writing, "I still think that, to the unprejudiced, the fossil record of plants is in favour of special creation." Ibid. Denton offers additional corroborative testimony noting, "The story is the same for plants. Again, the first representatives of each major group appear in the fossil record already highly specialized and highly characteristic of the group to which they belong. Perhaps one of the most abrupt arrivals of any plant group in the fossil record is the appearance of the angiosperms. . . . Like the sudden appearance of the first animal groups in the Cambrian rocks, the sudden appearance of the angiosperms is a persistent anomaly which has resisted all attempts at explanation since Darwin's time. . . . At their first appearance the angiosperms were divided into different classes, many of which have persisted with little change up to the present day." Denton, *Evolution*, 163.

what might one infer from the abrupt appearance of fully-formed, complex phyla with no evolutionary history whatsoever? One must account for the immediate appearance of such technological marvels. Is it not reasonable to consider the possibility of the work of a super intelligence?[18]

What other options exist? There is no evidence to suggest that it was a natural phenomenon generated by selection processes. So, if it didn't happen slowly, perhaps it happened fast. But how could this occur? The simplest answer, though repugnant to naturalists, seems to be that some-one designed them. This is nothing more than a logical inference made through observing the existing evidence. Even Gould conceded that based on the evidence alone, it appeared someone just put them there. The only reason such a conclusion is considered invalid is if one has ruled out such a possibility *a priori*. But this seems disingenuous, since, as we have seen, something supra-natural must have played a role in the causation of the universe. Thus one might reasonably infer that this something could also have played a role in populating the earth.

THE COMPLEXITY OF THE CELL

Biology is the study of complicated things that give the appearance of having been designed for a purpose.

Richard Dawkins, *The Blind Watchmaker*

Just as Darwin was mistaken about the fossil record, so he gravely mis-calculated the nature of cellular life. Today, thanks to the great advances made in genetics and biochemistry, Darwin's appeal to the simple cell could hardly be a greater misnomer. The simple cell, like the missing link, has been rendered obsolete in light of the vast complexity one discovers in the cell.[19]

18. William Dembski inquires, "With reference to biology, why should we have to constantly remind ourselves that biology studies things that only appear to be designed, but that in fact are not designed? Isn't it at least conceivable that there could be good posi-tive reasons for thinking biological systems are in fact designed?" Dembski, "Naturalism and Design," 256.

19. I restrict my discussion to the cell. But Michael Behe, Professor of biochemistry at Lehigh University, illuminates cellular activity within systems in his incisive work *Darwin's Black Box*. Behe's thesis is that many biochemical systems are irreducibly com-plex and thus could not have originated gradually in the prescribed Darwinian manner. Behe takes the reader into the world of cellular systems like the bacterial flagellum, the

Even the simplest cell is a miniature factory of immense sophistication, organization, and complexity. The technology of the cell far eclipses anything we can produce even in our most sophisticated computer programs and on a much, much smaller scale. The human body consists of trillions of such cells, each one busily at work in fulfilling its role to promote the greater good. Darwinism utterly fails in explaining the origin of the cell, since it operates on the assumption of life. At one time people thought the "simple cell" could be spontaneously generated if some amino acids and proteins interacted in a "primordial soup."

Today most reject such a notion as ludicrous due to the vast complexity and organization of cells. It would be a little like supposing that combining steel, glass, and rubber in a junkyard would randomly produce a Ferrari. Probability theory applied to cellular life creates a daunting challenge to any naturalistic explanation of life, making the chance assembly of this microscopic wonder virtually nil.[20]

---

cilium, and the blood clotting process among others. In each case, Behe argues that a number of highly sophisticated components are necessary in order for the system to be functional. In other words, unless each piece of the system is simultaneously present and complete, the system will not work. Thus gradualism cannot account for these highly technical, integrated biochemical systems, Behe argues.

20. Dembski's complexity/specification model urges the presence of design in biochemistry. He defines complexity in relation to probability in inverse order. In other words, the lower the probability the greater the complexity. He defines specification as "that which must be added to an otherwise highly improbable event in order to make chance an unacceptable" option. For instance, someone who flipped a coin one hundred times would produce an arrangement of heads and tails that would have been unlikely yet still retain the quality of chance—it just happened. But, if the sequence of heads and tails was specified in advance and then was actualized, Dembski argues, that would effectively eliminate chance as an option, making the event specified and highly complex. Another of his illustrations further clarifies the matter. He writes, "consider again a rat traversing a maze, but now take a very simple maze in which two right turns will conduct the rat out of the maze. How will a psychologist studying the rat determine if the rat has learned to exit the maze? Just putting the rat in the maze will not be enough. Because the maze is so simple, the rat could by chance just happen to take two right turns, and thereby exit the maze. The psychologist will therefore be uncertain whether the rat actually learned to exit the maze or whether the rat just got lucky. But contrast this now with a complicated maze in which the rat must take just the right sequence of left and right turns to exit the maze. Suppose the rat must take one hundred appropriate right and left turns, and that any mistake will prevent the rat from exiting the maze. A psychologist who sees the rat take no erroneous turns and in short order exit the maze will be convinced that the rat has indeed learned how to exit the maze, and that it was not dumb luck." Dembski argues that the immense sophistication and integration found in biochemical material more than satisfies complexity/specification criteria, mandating the presence of an intelligent

The DNA of a cell is the digital library of information, a library containing more organized information than the Encyclopedia Britannica; the RNA is the transport mechanism, providing the necessary information to the protein molecules, which actually do the work of assembling, folding, and transporting other proteins to the precise location in the body where and when they are needed. Stephen Meyer, PhD from Cambridge, calculates the odds of producing a single protein molecule by chance:

> First, you need the right bonds between the amino acids. Second, amino acids come in right-handed and left-handed versions, and you've got to get only left handed ones. Third, the amino acids must line up in a specified sequence, like letters in a sentence. Run the odds of those things falling into place on their own and you find that the probabilities of forming a rather short functional protein at random would be one chance in a hundred thousand trillion trillion trillion trillion trillion trillion trillion trillion trillion. That's a 10 with 125 zeroes after it![21]

designer. Dembski, "Naturalism and Design," 261, 272, and 273. Those wishing to read a more detailed and technical account of Dembski's argument should consult, Dembski, *The Design Inference.*

21. Meyer, "Evidence of Biological Information," 229. Consider the fact that proteins can require as many as two thousand letters or bases to form in exactly the correct order and be combined with precisely the correct amino acids and bonds in order to function. Furthermore, consider there are over 20,000 different kinds of proteins, each one calling for a different exact sequential arrangement of letters and bonds to accomplish their highly specific purpose. They are then transported by molecular machines to the exact place in the body where and when they are needed to fulfill the specific purpose for which they were built. If someone wishes to stake their destiny on the staggering odds of this sort of technological precision occurring randomly, no one can stop them. But as for me, I do not have that much faith in chance.

As Darwinist A.G. Cairns-Smith notes, "Ask any organic chemist how long it takes to put together a small protein, say one with 100 amino acids in it. Or go and look up the recipe for such an operation as it is written out in scientific journals. You will find pages and pages of tightly written instructions, couched in terms that assume your expertise in handling laboratory apparatus and require you to use many rather specialized and well-purified chemical reagents and solvents. And the result of following such instructions? If you are lucky a few thousandths of a gram of product from kilograms of starting materials." Cairns-Smith, *Seven Clues,* 29. Such complicated and technical directions suggest the need for an intelligent designer to produce this material—and a knowledgeable and highly skilled one at that.

For a technical and intriguing discussion regarding probability and evolution I recommend *Mathematical Challenges to the Neo-Darwinian Interpretation of Evolution,* Mooreland and Kaplan eds. I found the paper presented by Dr. Marcel Schutzenberger of particular interest. He writes "According to molecular biology, we have a space of objects (genotypes) endowed with nothing more than typographic topology. These objects cor-

And this, Meyer asserts, is what is required for a *single protein molecule* to form. Imagine the vast odds against producing a single cell by chance when one moderately complex cell requires from 300 to 500 protein molecules! That would be akin to suggesting that an explosion in a print shop could produce the Webster's dictionary or the Encyclopedia Britannica. Unbelievable! Absurd! Indeed, that's exactly the point.

The nature of cellular information is sophisticated and integrated, variable, bent on purpose. It is not basic and redundant; it is animated and vibrant. As the letters of the alphabet are diversely employed to articulate the thoughts of a writer and musical notes are variously arranged to express the mood of a composer, so is the information of a cell employed for diverse and varied purposes.

There are only twenty-six letters in the English alphabet but innumerable books, articles, stories, poems, etc. and there are only twelve musical notes (including sharps and flats) but thousands of different compositions. The letters and notes are organized and arranged in highly irregular

---

respond . . . with members of a second space having another typology. . . . Neo-Darwinism asserts that it is conceivable that without anything further, selection based upon the structure of the second space brings a statistically adapted drift when random changes are performed in the first space in accordance with its own structure. We believe that it is not conceivable. In fact, if we try to simulate such a situation . . . on computer programs we find that we have no chance (i.e. less than 1/101000) even to see what the modified program would compute; it just jams. . . . Thus no selection effected on the final output . . . would induce a drift, however slow, of the system towards the production of this mechanism if it were not already present in some form. Further, there is no chance (less than 10 to the thousandth power) to see this mechanism appear spontaneously and, if it did, even less for it to remain. . . . Thus, to conclude, we believe that there is a considerable gap in the neo-Darwinian theory of evolution, and we believe this gap to be of such a nature that it cannot be bridged within the current conception of biology." Schutzenberger, "Algorithms and Neo-Darwinian Theory," 74–75. The Chairman of the symposium held at the Wistar Institute of Anatomy and Biology, Dr. Waddington, clearly understood the significance of Schutzenberger's argument for in the period of discussion, at one point he stated, "Your argument is simply that life must have come about by special creation." Ibid., 80. This conclusion was denied by all concerned, but Waddington was right, it was the logical inference based on the daunting odds submitted against Darwinian evolution as an explanatory mechanism for the complexity of life. Waddington closed the symposium with the following comments: "I hope the biologists have shown the physicists that evolution theories are not *totally vacuous* [italics mine]. I think the physicists have shown us that they are certainly as yet very incomplete. Possibly we now know slightly better in which direction they are incomplete." Ibid., 102. I suspect that in the intervening passage of time (over 40 years since the Wistar Institute) and with the cataclysmic advances made in genetics and biochemistry, the highly improbable odds against Darwinian evolution have only become far worse.

patterns to fulfill the quest of the author or composer—the designing intelligence. The information in a cell is like that—flexible, variable, unpredictable, and brilliant. Indeed, the technology of the cell makes the most sophisticated human innovation appear primitive. To put it another way, if we know that a single shot musket is designed, we must know with far greater certitude that the same is true of a nuclear submarine.

But how did such advanced technological information enter the cell via naturalistic means or mechanisms? Naturalists have not even begun to formulate a coherent response to that inquiry—they are totally nonplussed. That is understandable since dead matter simply cannot produce brilliant intelligence. To materialists this mystery is truly insuperable. A better option is that it was intentionally developed and programmed. That would be consistent with our understanding of advanced technology.[22]

Keep in mind that Darwinians regularly concede the appearance of design in living things.[23] They acknowledge that living organisms look

22. Michael Behe illustrates the tendency of scientists to ignore the obvious: "Imagine a room in which a body lies crushed, flat as a pancake. A dozen detectives crawl around, examining the floor with magnifying glasses for any clue to the identity of the perpetrator. In the middle of the room, next to the body, stands a large gray elephant. The detectives carefully avoid bumping into the pachyderm's legs as they crawl, and never even glance at it. Over time the detectives get frustrated with their lack of progress but resolutely press on, looking even more closely at the floor. You see, textbooks say detectives must 'get their man,' so they never consider elephants. There is an elephant in the room full of scientists who are trying to explain the development of life. The elephant is labeled 'intelligent design.' To a person who does not feel obliged to restrict his search to unintelligent causes, the straightforward conclusion is that many biochemical systems were designed. They were designed, not by the laws of nature, not by chance and necessity; rather they were *planned*. The designer knew what the systems would look like when they were completed, then took steps to bring the systems about. Life on earth at its most fundamental level, in its most critical components, is the product of intelligent activity. The conclusion of intelligent design flows naturally from the data itself. . . ." Behe, *Darwin's Black Box*, 193. Behe comments further regarding the collective scientific research into cellular life, "The result of these cumulative efforts to investigate the cell—to investigate life at the molecular level—is a loud, clear, piercing cry of '*design*.' The result is so unambiguous and so significant that it must be ranked as one of the greatest achievements in the history of science. . . . Why does the scientific community not eagerly embrace its startling discovery? Why is the observation of design handled with intellectual gloves? The dilemma is that while one side of the elephant is labeled intelligent design, the other side might be labeled God. A non-scientist might ask an obvious question: so what?" Ibid., 232. In other words, if the evidence leads to such a conclusion, so be it.

23. Cairns-Smith admits, "After all what impresses us about a living thing is its inbuilt ingenuity, its appearance of having been designed, thought-out—of having been put together with a purpose." Cairns-Smith, *Seven Clues*, quoted in P. Johnson, *Darwin*

like they are the product of a designing intelligence, so it isn't as though creationists are making it up. However, Darwinists go on to argue that this characteristic is merely illusionary not actual. But why do they urge this conclusion? What evidence do they possess to contradict what seems so patently obvious?

Their bias is their evidence. It is philosophy, not empiricism, that mandates their position.[24] So on the one hand naturalists admit that living organisms appear designed. They then dismiss this clear observation based on their prejudicial bias, ridiculing empiricists who choose to submit to the logical inferences of the evidence rather than to the philo-

---

on Trial, 109–10. Cairns-Smith further puzzles as he confronts the complexity of cellular activity: "[I]t is not just the need for enzymes, here, there, and everywhere; it is not just that enzymes are of little use unless they have been made properly; it is not just that ribosomes are so very sophisticated—and look as though they would have to be to do their job; . . . There seems also to be a more fundamental difficulty. Any conceivable kind of organism would have to contain messages of some sort and equipment for reading and reprinting the messages; any conceivable organism would thus seem to have to be packed with machinery and as such need a miracle (or something) for the first of its kind to have appeared. That's the problem." Cairns-Smith, *Seven Clues*, 30.

24. The candid remarks of Harvard biologist Richard Lewontin are a case in point: "Our willingness to accept scientific claims that are against common sense is the key to an understanding of the real struggle between science and the supernatural. We take the side of science *in spite* of the patent absurdity of some of its constructs, *in spite* of its failure to fulfill many of its extravagant promises of health and life, *in spite* of the tolerance of the scientific community for unsubstantiated just-so stories, because we have a prior commitment, a commitment to materialism. It is not that the methods and institutions of science somehow compel us to accept a material explanation of the phenomenal world, but, on the contrary, that we are forced by our *a priori* adherence to material causes to create an apparatus of investigation and a set of concepts that produce material explanations, no matter how counterintuitive, no matter how mystifying to the uninitiated. Moreover, that materialism is absolute, for we cannot allow a divine foot in the door." Lewontin, "Billions and Billions of Demons," 31.

For materialists, their philosophy must prevail no matter how paltry or contradictory the evidence. But if science starts with facts and then formulates theories based upon them, this model seems grossly inverted. And if theists are considered tainted because of an *a priori* belief in God, why are not materialists equally tainted due to their *a priori* commitment to atheism? Both inevitably end up making "God claims." Instead of hypocritically muzzling design advocates, why not permit both in the debate—and *assess the arguments based on their merit as measured against the evidence.* The double standard that currently prevails in education is intellectually irresponsible. If "God talk" is proscribed then this censure should apply equally to those who speak for and those who speak against God. Materialism is not the necessary consequence of scientific experimentation; it is a philosophical worldview—dignified with scientific credentials by vague allusions to scientific methods.

sophical bias of naturalism. This is convoluted reasoning on their part and intellectually irresponsible.[25]

Darwinians often write and speak as though they have captured the intellectual high ground, belittling people who think a designer had something to do with creation.[26] But after an inspection of the evidence, it seems Darwinists are the ones living in the world of make-believe. Their story requires hordes of phantom creatures which have never been observed, its predictions are incorrect concerning the fossil evidence and the nature of the cell, it bestows fantastical creative powers upon natural selection without warrant, its claims are rendered untenable by probability theory—beyond all reason, it offers no explanatory mechanism for the origin of life or the presence of brilliant technology inside dead chemicals. The evidence for the grand Darwinian claim is meager at best. Only those thoroughly committed to the philosophy of naturalism can possibly feel satisfied with such discouraging support.

To my mind, theism is a far more compelling option in explaining the universe, our world, and us. Far from fantasy, such a conviction is the product of inference and deduction through observation. The circum-

---

25. Dembski argues that effective criteria for determining design exist via the complexity-specification model. He concludes his argument writing, "There is no principled way of excluding design from the causal structure of the world.... Naturalism is therefore seen to be false on strictly scientific grounds. The logic of this conclusion is straightforward: naturalism allows only certain sorts of fundamental causes (chance and necessity). Those causes are (demonstrably) incapable of generating specified complexity. But nature exhibits specified complexity, especially in biology. Therefore, naturalism is false." Dembski, "Naturalism and Design," 277.

26. Patronizing comments like these of Dawkins are typical: "Pretend as they will to scientific credentials, the anti-evolution propagandists are always religiously motivated, even if they try to buy credibility by concealing the fact. In most cases, they know deep down what to believe because their parents recommended an ancient book that tells them what to believe. If the scientific evidence learned in adulthood contradicts the book, there must be something wrong with the scientific evidence.... The holy book of childhood cannot, *must* not be wrong." Dawkins, *Blind Watchmaker*, xi. Apparently, Dawkins does not believe one can be religious and possess authentic credentials. This is as insulting as it is inaccurate. He disqualifies scientists who are religious because their motives are allegedly sullied. Why, one wonders, are not zealous atheists like Dawkins equally disqualified. Both are advocating about God, one for and the other against. Both are making inferences based upon the actual evidence. His tactics are typical of evolutionists who want to silence dissent by belittling their opponents. Contrary to his assertion, many who find Darwinism unpersuasive hold excellent credentials from outstanding universities. In my own case, I completed the PhD in history from the University of Rochester in four years, earning three academic prizes along the way.

stantial evidence suggesting a superintelligence—a Designer, a Creator—is compelling. For instance, all our experience and knowledge informs us that organized, complex information, such as in the cell, is always and invariably the product of intelligence. This is never falsified.

So to deduce that the cell is the product of a designing intelligence is in harmony with everything we know about sophisticated information and technology. To argue otherwise contradicts everything we know, placing enormous amounts of faith in random chance without warrant. Theism and atheism are not intellectual equals. The former is logical and the other is not, one is in harmony with all we know and the other abruptly contradicts all we know. Thus I contend that theism is simply the more compelling model—logically and rationally superior because it harmonizes better with the evidence.

As one approaches our town across the bridge to the west, one encounters a floral sign on a hillside that says, "Welcome to Webster." No sane person would believe even for a moment that the sign was the product of random forces and chance across time. But this is merely sixteen characters and two spaces—hardly advanced calculus. Nonetheless, we know intuitively that it was designed. The characters are put together intentionally to communicate a message. If reason refuses to accept that this simple sign was the product of chance, why in the world would anyone accept such a conclusion when considering the technological brilliance and sophistication of a cell?[27]

One might ask: If all this is true, why do so many people believe in Darwinism? After all, most biologists believe in it and the National Academy of Science endorses it—with religious vigor. How could they be wrong? Well, keep in mind that truth is not the product of majority rule.[28]

27. "Mutation and selection are incapable of generating the highly specific, complex, information-rich structures in nature that signal not merely apparent but actual design—that is, intelligent design. Organisms display the hallmarks of intelligently engineered high-tech systems: information storage and transfer; functioning codes; sorting and delivery systems; self-regulation and feed-back loops; signal transduction circuitry; and everywhere, complex arrangements of mutually-interdependent and well-fitted parts that work in concert to perform a function. For this reason, University of Chicago molecular biologist James Shapiro, who refuses to count himself as a design theorist, regards Darwinism as almost completely unenlightening for understanding biological complexity and prefers an information processing model. Design theorists take this one step further, arguing that information processing presupposes a programmer." Dembski and Kushiner, *Signs of Intelligence*, 11.

28. History is strewn with the remnants of flawed thinking which received major-

I suspect part of the answer resides in the fact that many secularists hold very strong prior commitments to the philosophy of naturalism. Thus their worldview is essentially impregnable against particular criticisms of Darwinian theory. They reason that though the support may be tenuous, the model must be true. Since they have ruled out *a priori* any other possible resolution, naturalism, by default, must provide the answer. But in concluding thus it becomes apparent that their allegiance is more to a philosophy than to empiricism. Hence when the evidence and the philosophy diverge, they loyally follow the philosophy.

Furthermore, they are programmed to seek out support for a theory they *already know* to be true. That is a treacherous model for intellectual inquiry as we shall see. In such an insulated environment, small consequences are hailed as compelling proofs. For instance, minor variation among species is a commonly accepted observable fact, as with Darwin's finches or as between a poodle and a German shepherd. Darwinists believe that such modest modifications within species represent concrete evidence for macro-evolutionary transmutations—the development of entirely new species. Of course, the logical obstacle for such extrapolation is that small variation within species is observable but the development of new species is not. Indeed, the fossil record testifies that it never has occurred.

To those who retain even a modicum of objectivity, the fact that beak length varies among finches based on environment does not even begin to address basic issues like where birds originally came from to begin with. To the candid mind, such things have literally nothing to do with the question of origin of life and the development of species. But in many secular institutions, if one intends to earn a PhD in biology one must pledge allegiance to Darwinian naturalism. The "fact of evolution" is assumed, eliminating nagging questions and dodging inconsistencies while perpetuating the myth. However, even in the midst of substantial pressure to conform, biologists who disavow Darwinism represent a growing minority.[29] But is it really possible that such a distinguished group of intellectuals could be so wrong? Regrettably, it would not be the first time.

---

ity approval at the time. It is not what we believe that is primary but why we believe it. Argument is of the highest moment—and I simply find the Darwinian argument unconvincing.

29. The sophistication of the machinery found in the cell led biophysicist Professor Dean Kenyon to reject the thesis of his own influential book, *Biological Predestination*, as

BIOLOGICAL RACISM:
A CASE STUDY OF PSEUDO SCIENCE

The improvement of our stock seems to me one of the highest objects that we can reasonably attempt. . . . I see no impossibility of Eugenics becoming a religious dogma among mankind.

Francis Galton, founder of eugenics

From the mid-nineteenth century until the close of World War II, the science of craniology was at the forefront of intellectual inquiry in Europe and America. Many scientists argued that intellectual capacity could be effectively determined via brain volume. Thus the size of the skull was considered a reliable indicator of mental capacity.[30] The scientist and stat-

---

inadequate to explain the technological brilliance of the cell. Kenyon had hoped to find some self-ordering tendency among amino acids that would explain the attraction of acids and proteins naturally. The effort proved futile. And even if such a tendency had been found, would it not merely produce redundant bonds rather than the kind of variable, irregular, and unpredictable organization characteristic of the cell? Professor Kenyon wrote an endorsement for a creation science book in which he states, "If after reading this book carefully and reflecting on its argument one still prefers the evolutionary view, or still contends that the creationist view is religion and the evolutionary view is pure science, he should ask himself whether something other than the facts of nature is influencing his thinking about origins." Morris and Parker, *What is Creation Science?* back cover. Kenyon comments regarding macroevolution, the transmutation of one species into another: "All changes observed in the laboratory and the breeding pen are limited. They represent microevolution, not macroevolution. These limited changes do not accumulate the way Darwinian evolutionary theory requires in order to produce macro changes. . . . A commonly accepted definition of species is an interbreeding population with fertile offspring. . . . Yet even speciation represents only limited change. Stickleback fish may diversify into fresh-water dwellers and salt-water dwellers, but both remain sticklebacks. One fruit fly may breed on apple trees and another on hawthorn trees, but both remain fruit flies. Speciation is a means of creating diversity within types of living things, but macroevolution is much more than diversity. Macroevolution requires an increase in the gene pool, the addition of new genetic information, whereas the means to speciation . . . represent the loss of genetic information." Davis and Kenyon, *Of Pandas and People*, 12 and 19.

30. For those wishing to investigate this more thoroughly through primary sources, I suggest the following as helpful starting points: Arthur de Gobineau, *Inequality of Human Races*, and Francis Galton, *Hereditary Genius*. "Comte Arthur de Gobineau (1816–1882) was not an original thinker, but a synthesizer who drew on anthropology, linguistics, and history in order to construct a fully furnished intellectual edifice where race explained everything in the past, present, or future. . . . His *Essay on the Inequality of Human Races* . . . spelled out his racism in awesome detail and was based upon the best scholarship then available." Mosse, *Final Solution*, 51. This work provides an interesting history of the

istician Francis Galton developed the science of eugenics which sought to improve the human species through selective breeding. Through the influence of eugenics, thousands of people in America were sterilized because they were deemed unfit to reproduce. Furthermore, biological racism played a role in United States immigration laws established in the 1920s, seeking to limit the influx of "undesirables." In Germany eugenics was known as Rassenhygiene—or race hygiene.[31]

Leading thinkers like Galton, Samuel Morton, Robert Bean, Franz Josef Gall, Georges Cuvier, and Paul Broca among many others, believed in a hierarchy of races and that measurements of the skull provided conclusive quantitative evidence for their convictions.[32] The hierarchy consistently assigned the highest intellectual rating to white European males, and then with some modest variations, came women, Native Americans, Eskimos, and Blacks, who frequently occupied the lowest rung in the models. Not surprisingly, those conducting the experiments were white European males.

But prior bias played no role in their investigative work, they urged. They simply followed the facts to their inevitable conclusions.[33] Broca vowed that he operated by a key axiom of science: facts must precede theories.[34] They measured the actual skulls of the deceased using various techniques like filling the skull with lead shot, measuring the circumference, or by weighing it. All indications suggest that Broca was meticu-

---

development of biological racism.

31. Galton, "Eugenics: Its Definition Scope and Aims," in Hackett, *Idea of Race*, 79. This book offers a nice introduction to some important literature regarding the concept of race and racial identity and hierarchy.

32. "Franz Joseph Gall's (1758–1828) phrenology added a pseudo-scientific dimension to the reading of faces. Gall's basic notion was that character could be read through the configuration of the head. Phrenology rested on three principles: that the brain was the organ of the mind; that the brain was composed of a variety of organs, each of which had a specific function; and finally that the brain shaped the skull." Thus he argued that intellectual capabilities could be properly judged by the shape of the human skull. Mosse, *Final Solution*, 27.

33. Gould, *Mismeasure of Man*, 114–40. I am indebted to Professor Gould for his translation and analysis of the work of Paul Broca and for his incisive book, particularly his chapter "Measuring Heads," 105–41, from which I have gleaned much helpful material. I first encountered this dark episode of intellectual history as a PhD student at the University of Rochester.

34. Ibid., 116.

lously careful in his quantification. This fact separated him from some hastier scientists like Robert Bennett Bean.

Bean conducted his experiments using skulls from the cadavers of both Whites and Blacks. He developed a technique of measuring the genu and splenium or the anterior and posterior areas of the corpus callosum. It was commonly believed that the front portion, the genu, held the intellectual components and the splenium, the posterior part, contained elements related to emotions and feelings. His research included scores of skulls from both white and black individuals, and he discovered an overwhelming, irrefutable correlation. Those belonging to white people had a much larger genu than those of blacks and hence a far greater capacity for intelligence. Conversely the posterior region, (the splenium) was substantially larger in the black population, meaning that blacks were more capricious, less reliable, and more emotional than white people.[35]

However, Bean's mentor at Johns Hopkins, Franklin Mall, repeated Bean's analysis some while later, using the very same specimens as those employed by Bean. There was, however, one important variable. Mall conducted his experiments anonymously. In other words, he had no idea which skull came from a white person or a black person. Bean had labeled them. What did Mall discover? He found that there was absolutely no measurable variance between the two groups. Bean had either consciously or unconsciously manipulated the numbers in order to achieve the anticipated and desired results. Unfortunately, Bean's spurious results were published in popular form, becoming conventional wisdom and spurring some to suggest abandoning public education for black people as a hopeless cause.

But even those who exercised considerable caution in experimentation were prone to the same sort of biased analysis. Broca, like most of his colleagues, expected that brain capacity would increase over time based upon evolution. He earned acclaim for his work demonstrating that European civilization had advanced intellectually from the medieval period forward. In order to conduct the experiment, he had hundreds of samples exhumed from three cemeteries in Paris dating from the twelfth, eighteenth, and nineteenth centuries. His expectation was that the skulls would become progressively larger as brain capacity increased over time. However, the evidence appeared to refute this expectation.

35. Ibid., 109.

In chronological order, from earliest to latest, the brain capacities measured 1,426, 1,409, and 1,462 cc. How could the twelfth-century specimens be larger than the eighteenth-century ones? Broca attributed this discrepancy to social class, arguing that the earlier skulls had been collected from a churchyard. Thus they represented the aristocracy of the period; while the eighteenth-century skulls came from a common grave, representing the lowest strata of society—and everyone knows, Broca reasoned, that the elite in society are more intelligent than others. Thus Broca argued it was an unfair comparison, in that the elite of the twelfth century were compared to inferior specimens—the dregs of eighteenth-century society.

But this tampering with the evidence did not solve the entire problem for Broca because he had samples from the nineteenth century coming from both common graves and individual graves. The common grave was used to inter the poor collectively, while individual graves were reserved for those with the means to pay (i.e., the elite). The ninety samples from individual graves of the nineteenth century averaged a measurement of 1484. Thirty-five additional samples had come from common graves and averaged 1403. Why, Broca puzzled, did the specimens from common graves of the eighteenth century measure slightly larger than those from the nineteenth century?

Rather than questioning the validity of his assumptions and prior commitments, Broca pressed on, rationalizing as he went. Gould observes:

> But Broca was not to be defeated; he argued that the eighteenth-century common grave included a better class of people. In these pre-revolutionary times, a man had to be really rich or noble to rest in a churchyard. The dregs of the poor measured 1403 in the nineteenth century; the dregs leavened by good stock yielded about the same value one hundred years before.[36]

One is left with the uneasy impression that Broca handled the evidence with something less than full candor—consciously or otherwise. He twisted the facts to fit his preconceived idea. Gould's assessment of this dark period is that the researchers began with their convictions already

---

36. Ibid., 128. Gould further quipped that this, "probably represents the best case of hope dictating conclusions that I have ever encountered." Ibid., 127. I suspect that Darwinism is a close contemporary rival.

established then used "facts" to prove what they already knew to be true. Contrary to Broca's claim, it is obvious that his theory was thoroughly entrenched before the first "fact" was ever considered and consequently he saw only what he expected to see.

They did not use the facts to construct their theory; they used selective evidence to prop it up. If something didn't fit preconceived ideas, they simply discarded it as unimportant or irrelevant.[37] This sort of bogus experimentation only worked within an intellectual and social context of shared desires—the quantification of the superiority of Whites and the inferiority of Blacks. However, no such quantification ever existed. Looking back, we consider it absurd that anyone could have ever believed such drivel. Yet this was the intellectual establishment—the academy— elite scientists. It is a sobering historical reminder that the "facts" do not necessarily tell the story, the storytellers do.[38]

37. For instance, Broca employed experiments using the "ratio of radius (lower arm bone) to humerous (upper arm bone), reasoning that a higher ratio marks a longer forearm—a characteristic of apes." However, when such calculations placed whites lower in rank than some brown-skinned groups, Broca decided that this characteristic had no force in assessing superiority or inferiority. Rather than question his assumption, he simply abandoned the criteria as useless. Gould, *Mismeasure*, 118–9. In Robert Bean's experiment discussed above, he failed to note the total measurements of the skull, focusing his attention instead on the genu and splenium. One wonders why, since total cranial size was believed to indicate intellectual capacity. The answer is buried in notes—their was no difference in total skull size. Thus, Bean had to change the conditions of the test to acquire results he considered desirable.

38. I discovered the truth of this principle while researching my first book, *The Sacred Text*, in which I examined the position of the Protestant theological elite in America concerning their view of the Bible. A prevailing point of view popularized by Ernest Sandeen had argued that the doctrine of biblical inerrancy was actually a new innovation with its genesis out of Princeton Theological Seminary, emerging in the late nineteenth century. Sandeen asserted that Princeton theologians conjured up the doctrine in order to insulate the Bible from increasing critical inspection. Theological liberals from 1970 forward had, generally, readily accepted Sandeen's influential theory, marginalizing inerrancy and those who endorsed it as decidedly out of concert with mainstream Protestant thinking. But, my research revealed that this is incorrect. Mainline Protestant leaders throughout the nineteenth century considered the doctrine of biblical inerrancy as an essential tenet to orthodoxy. This was true of Congregationalists, Presbyterians, Baptists, and Methodists. Any attempt to sequester inerrancy to Princeton Seminary is hopeless in light of the abundant evidence to the contrary. In point of fact, it was the liberals who were the innovators. I suspect that Sandeen's argument was embraced, not because of its coherence, but because of its convenience. It gave liberals a plausible, if less than thorough, argument relegating conservative Protestants to the intellectual and theological backwaters. But the evidence I uncovered condemned this widely accepted theory as

What brought this period of intellectual nonsense to a close? It was World War II. Hitler's Germany represented the horrific apex of racist thinking justified by the pseudo science of biological determinism. Following liberation of the concentration camps and the firsthand observation of the carnage such twisted thinking had wrought; the hierarchy of races idea fell from popular favor. It is significant to note that its demise came not via the elite but from the grassroots. It had become such a repugnant idea that the majority of people simply stopped believing it. During WWII, black and white soldiers had fought courageously, effectively, and with great honor, though in segregated groups. President Harry S. Truman desegregated the military before the Korean War and the long, hard road to Civil Rights was under construction though not without many obstacles, detractors, and challenges.

During one of my lectures on early American history and religion at Brockport College, one of my students asked me directly my opinion on the creation/evolution controversy. I was happy to respond to his question, stating that I did not believe in evolution and that I endorsed creation. Eyes bulged, jaws fell open, pencils dropped. The lecture hall filled with more than 100 students was quiet.

I went on to briefly state that I had good reasons for my position and I was certain they had good reasons for their position. I smiled as I answered; but I did not blink, I did not blush, I did not feel the least bit uncomfortable because I am convinced theism is the most compelling option. We then returned to American history. After class, some students came forward to thank me for sharing my position; they shared it as well.[39]

Perhaps the time has come for theists to stand more openly and collectively against an idea that, to my mind, is something akin to an assault on reason. Maybe we need to practice intellectual resistance by politely

---

entirely false. See Satta, *The Sacred Text*.

39. "Indeed, Gallup Polls consistently indicate that only about 10 percent of the population of the United States accepts the sort of evolution advocated by Dawkins . . . that is, evolution in which the driving force is the Darwinian selection mechanism. The rest of the population is committed to some form of intelligent design. . . . Why has the biological community failed to convince the public that natural selection is the driving force behind evolution and that evolution so conceived . . . can successfully account for the full diversity of life? . . . I submit that the real reason the public continues to resist Darwinian evolution is because the Darwinian mechanism of chance variation and natural selection seems inadequate to account for the full diversity of life." Dembski and Kushiner, *Signs of Intelligence*, 14–15. Indeed, entirely inadequate.

but candidly expressing our disapproval of Darwinism—that we simply find its argument unconvincing. Of course this will produce some measure of hostility, but what would have come of the Civil Rights movement if its participants had run from controversy?[40]

40. Percival Davis and Dean Kenyon produced a fascinating, fair, and thought-provoking supplemental science textbook called *Of Pandas and People*. They observe, "How do we decide if something is the result of natural or intelligent causes? Most of us do it without even thinking. We see clouds and we know, based on our experience, they are the result of natural causes. No matter how intricate the shapes may be, we know that a cloud is simply water vapor shaped by the wind and the temperature. On the other hand, we may see something looking very much like a cloud that spells out the words 'Vote for Smedley.' We know that, even though they are white and fluffy like clouds, the words cannot be the result of natural causes. Why not? Because our experience—and that of everybody else—tells us that natural causes do not give rise to complex structures such as linguistic messages. When we find 'John loves Mary' written in the sand, we assume it resulted from an intelligent cause. Experience is the basis for science as well. When we find a complex message coded into the nucleus of a cell, it is reasonable to draw the same conclusion. . . . In other words when scientists probed the nucleus of the cell, they eventually stumbled upon a phenomenon akin to finding 'John loves Mary' written in the sand, or 'Vote for Smedley' written in the sky. The greatest difference is that the DNA text is much more complex. If the amount of information in one cell of your body were written out . . . it would fill as many books as are contained in a large library. Are natural causes capable of producing these kinds of patterns? To say that DNA and protein arose by natural causes, as chemical evolution does, is to say complex, coded messages arose by natural causes. It is akin to saying 'John loves Mary' arose from the action of the waves, or from the interaction of the grains of sand. It is like saying the painting of a sunset arose spontaneously from the atoms in the paint and the canvas. When in our experience have we ever witnessed such an event? Whenever we recognize a sequence as meaningful symbols we assume it is the handiwork of some intelligent cause. . . . If science is based upon experience, then science tells us the message encoded in DNA must have originated from an intelligent cause." Davis and Kenyon, *Of Pandas and People*, 7.

The fact that this book was deemed inadmissible to public education because its authors held religious convictions, suggests, to my mind, a materialistic monopoly in education, one which more closely resembles religious dogmatism than intellectual enlightenment. One wonders when common sense became criminal. Should theists (the vast majority of Americans) be afforded the opportunity to investigate the ideological backgrounds of all scientific textbook writers? Perhaps some of them have strongly held anti-God sentiments which might induce them into making all kinds of unwarranted "God claims" in the classroom. The fact is that such witch hunting is totally irrelevant to the case. What matters is one's argument—not one's ideological convictions—religious or otherwise. The fact remains that many intelligent and well-credentialed individuals find the Darwinian argument seriously flawed and far from persuasive. Many of these people contend that design/theism is more compelling based upon the evidence. Thus, it seems more fair, more democratic, and intellectually responsible to make all the evidence and dominant arguments accessible to people, allowing them to critically assess the persuasive value of each. If Darwinism is scientifically valid, as its advocates con-

The debate should always be conducted with civility, courtesy, and respect for all sides. After all, in a democracy such as ours, everyone has the right to believe whatever one finds convincing. Theism, as a natural consequence of inference and deduction through observation, should clearly be one of the major options admitted to the discussion. Only in tyrannies are ideas stifled, suppressed, and silenced. Ideas should prevail on their merit not through intimidation, manipulation, and force.

Darwinists will retort that such resistance will paralyze the forward progress of science. Nonsense. This assertion is nothing but a scare tactic. Anyone who has even a fundamental grasp on history knows very well that the vast majority of the pioneers of science were dedicated theists.[41] Rather than blunt scientific inquiry, theism incited the quest for

---

tend, it should survive and perhaps even prevail. If it is not, it should be exposed. But, in either case, people should have access to the whole story not just the carefully edited version. As Davis and Kenyon write, "*Pandas* helps students understand the positive case for intelligent design. Following a growing number of scientists and philosophers, the authors argue that life not only *appears* to have been intelligently designed but that it actually was. Drawing on recent developments in molecular biology, the authors show that even simple organisms bear all the earmarks of designed systems. . . . By presenting the case for intelligent design the authors demonstrate that there are alternatives to the blind watchmaker thesis—and that evolution as a purposeless process is neither an indisputable fact nor the only inference supported by biological data." *Pandas,* 157. I was under the impression that education strives to teach critical thinking skills to students not simply indoctrinate them. Indeed, I have argued that the case for design is simply superior—more cogent, logical, and compelling than that of its rival. But then, perhaps this is precisely what Darwinians fear.

41. "There is, I shall argue, no contradiction between holding a staunch belief in supernatural design and being a creative scientist, and perhaps no one illustrates this point better than the seventeenth-century astronomer Johannes Kepler. He was one of the most creative astronomers of all time, a man who played a major role in bringing about the acceptance of the Copernican system through his efficacy of his tables of planetary motion. Now one of the principal reasons Kepler was a Copernican arose from his deeply held belief that the sun-centered arrangement reflected the divine design of the cosmos: the sun at the center was the image of God, the outer surface of the star-studded heavenly sphere was the image of Christ, and the intermediate planetary space represented the Holy Spirit. These were not ephemeral notions of his student years, but a constant obsession that inspired and drove him throughout his entire life. Today Kepler is best remembered for his discovery of the elliptical form of the planets' orbits.

This discovery and another, the so-called law of areas, are chronicled in his *Astronomia Nova,* truly the New Astronomy. In his introduction he defended his Copernicanism from the point of view that the heavens declare the glory of God. . . . Kepler's life and works provide central evidence that an individual can be both a creative scientist and a believer in divine design in the universe, and that indeed the very motivation for the scientific research can stem from a desire to trace God's handiwork. In the centuries that followed,

discovery.[42]

In this chapter, I have argued that theism is the most compelling option in explaining the universe, our world, and us. The observable circumstantial evidence suggests the existence of a powerful, brilliant, and benevolent Designer. This evidence does not negate the need for faith. Indeed, faith is an important and necessary corollary for either theism or atheism. But, in the Bible, faith is contrasted with sight not with reason. I contend that theism is true beyond a reasonable doubt.

But what about the Designer? Is it possible to identify this powerful, brilliant, and benevolent Creator? I think it is. I contend that Christianity likely holds the answers. But why would I suggest such a thing? It is to that question we now turn.

many scientists took inspiration from the idea that the heavens declared the glory of God, but God's hand appeared less and less in their physical explanations. In a sense, one of the fundamental consequences of the scientific revolution . . . was the secularization of the natural world. . . . Nevertheless, random opportunism (as opposed to design) has been raised to such a level of scientific orthodoxy that some of our contemporaries forget that this is just a tactic of science, an assumption, and not a guaranteed principle of reality." Gingerich, "Dare a Scientist Believe?" 28–30.

42. Dembski asserts, "Design is not a science-stopper. Indeed design can foster inquiry where traditional evolutionary approaches obstruct it. . . . Design encourages scientists to look for function where evolution discourages it (regarding DNA). Or consider vestigial organs that later are found to have a function after all. Evolutionary biology texts often cite the human coccyx as a 'vestigial structure' that harkens back to vertebrate ancestors with tails. Yet if one looks at a recent addition of *Gray's Anatomy*, one finds that the coccyx is a crucial point of contact with muscles that attach to the pelvic floor. . . . Thus here again we find design encouraging scientists to look for function where evolution discourages it. Examples where the phrase 'vestigial structure' merely cloaks our current lack of knowledge about function can be multiplied. The human appendix, formerly thought to be vestigial, is now known to be a functioning component of the immune system. Admitting design into science can only enrich science." Dembski, *Signs of Intelligence*, 276. As helpful as such a model might be to scientific inquiry, Dembski realizes that its implications are more far-reaching: "Even so, design does much more than enrich and transform science. Indeed, design has profound metaphysical and world-view implications." Ibid.

2

Scripture: The Most Reliable Source

T HE EVIDENCE CLEARLY INDICATES that the ancient church, the Reformation church, and the post-Reformation churches aligned concerning their view of Scripture, endorsing biblical inerrancy as essential orthodoxy. Key representatives from these periods believed that the Bible, rightly interpreted and in the original autographs, was divinely inspired and completely reliable in everything to which it spoke whether pertaining to matters of faith or fact, right down to the very words.[1]

1. For a fuller discussion of the inerrancy of the original autograph doctrine see Satta, *The Sacred Text*. Theologian John Dick is representative of this opinion having written in 1800: "While we admire the care of Divine Providence in the preservation of the scriptures, we do not affirm that all the transcribers of them were miraculously guarded against all error. Various motives . . . contributed to render them scrupulously careful; but that they were under no infallible guidance, is evident from the different readings, which are discovered by a collation of manuscripts, and the mistakes in matters of greater or less importance, observable in them all. A contradiction, which could not be imputed to the blunder of a transcriber, but was fairly chargeable on the sacred writers themselves, would completely disprove their inspiration." Dick, *Essay on Inspiration*, 186–87. Several important deductions are observed: first, infallible guidance was attributed only to the sacred penmen, not to copyists; second, the sacred penmen made no mistake, thus the need to attribute blunders to the transcribers; third, inspiration demanded perfection in the text of the original; thus a true error attributable to the original writer would disprove inspiration. The comments of nineteenth-century biblical scholar D.A. Whedon are indicative of the intense commitment commonly ascribed to verbal inspiration and the errorless quality of the original, divinely inspired text. He stated, "Biblical criticism aims at ascertaining the precise words of Holy Scripture as they stood in the original autographs of the sacred writers. Those words were true, authoritative, inspired. . . . The labor is to ascertain the exact language, even to the insertion of an article, the orthography of a word, the inflection of a noun, the mood and tense of a verb, so that we shall have 'the words which the Holy Ghost teacheth.'" Whedon, "Greek Text of the New Testament," 325. Neither are these isolated comments but are simply illustrative of that which pervades the scholarly literature of the nineteenth century in America. See for instance: Woods, *Lectures on the Inspiration of the Scriptures*, 88 and 92; Alexander, "Review of Woods on Inspiration," 18; Lee, *Inspiration of Holy Scripture*, 337; Pond, review of *Inspiration of Holy*

Now obviously just because some ancient people believed such a thing, is no compelling reason for anyone else to do so. Every religion has its zealots. Nonetheless, it is worth identifying what they considered orthodoxy regarding the Bible. After this is accomplished, we will explore more fully *why* they believed such a thing, assessing the character of the Bible to test its reliability.

THE ORTHODOX OPINION OF THE BIBLE

From among the earliest church fathers one finds testimony to the divine nature of Scripture and the errorless quality they anticipated from the sacred writings of the inspired penmen. Irenaeus (130–200), writing in *Against Heresies*, explicitly ascribed perfection to the Scriptures as a necessary corollary of their source—deity. He wrote in this regard, "being most properly assured that the Scriptures are indeed perfect, since they were spoken by the Word of God and His Spirit."[2] They considered canonical literature flawless and entirely reliable. What other quality could a divine composition exhibit. After all, how could God make a mistake?

Comments such as those by Irenaeus led even nineteenth-century critics of inerrancy to concede that it in fact represented orthodoxy in the early church. William Sanday, Professor of exegesis at Exeter College Oxford, made just such a concession in 1893, noting:

> Testimonies to the general doctrine of inspiration may be multiplied to almost any extent; but there are some which go further and point to an inspiration which might be described as "verbal." Nor does this idea come in tentatively and by degrees, but almost from the very first. Both Irenaeus and Tertullian regard inspiration as determining the choice of particular words and phrases. . . . Tertullian like Irenaeus, quite adopts the formula of St. Matthew and other New Testament writers as to the Spirit of God speaking "through" the human author. . . . We cannot wonder if this high doctrine sometimes takes the form of asserting the absolute perfection and infallibility of the Scriptures. We saw that Irenaeus attributes to the apostles "perfect knowledge." Elsewhere he is still more explicit, asserting that the Scriptures

---

Scripture, 33 and 53; Torrey and Burlington, "Essay on Inspiration," 334; "Geographical Accuracy of the Bible," 451–2 and 463; Robinson, "Rawlinson's Historical Evidences," 505, 510–1; C. Hodge, review of *Inspiration of Holy Scripture*, 674–5; and Lord, "Inspiration of the Scriptures," 25.

2. Roberts and Donaldson, *Ante-Nicene Fathers*, 1:399.

must needs be "perfect, as having been spoken by the Word of God and His Spirit."[3]

This candid admission by a stern critic of inerrancy is compelling evidence in favor of its historical legitimacy. Indeed, throughout the writings of the church fathers one regularly encounters comments attributing a divine character to canonical literature. The early fathers operated under the assumption that the Word was the product of divine generation and completely trustworthy when accurately interpreted. Augustine of Hippo (345–430), one of the most influential leaders of the fifth-century church, echoed similar sentiments noting, "Indeed, all of us who read (Scripture) endeavor to trace out and to understand that which he whom we read wished to convey; and as we believe him to speak truly, we dare not suppose that he has spoken anything which we either know or suppose to be false."[4]

Athanasius (296–373), Bishop of Alexandria, clearly identified the books that the church had accepted within the sacred canon. He did so in an Easter letter. In explaining the expediency of such a project he wrote:

> For as much as some have taken in hand, to reduce into order for themselves the books termed apocryphal, and to mix them up with the divinely inspired Scriptures, concerning which we have been fully persuaded, as they who from the beginning were eye

---

3. Sanday, *Inspiration*, 34–37. During the nineteenth century traditional biblical orthodoxy was assailed by several challengers, among them the newly emerging science of geology, Darwinism, textual criticism, and theological liberalism.

4. Schaff and Wace, *Nicene and Post-Nicene Fathers*, 1:183. It may have been precisely this ancient text that influenced an important Reformation scholar when he wrote, "We cannot but wholly disapprove of the opinion of those who think that the sacred writers have, in some places, fallen into mistakes. That some of the ancients were of this opinion appears from the testimony of Augustine, who maintains, in opposition to them, 'that the evangelists are free from all falsehood, both from that which proceeds from deliberate deceit and that which is the result of forgetfulness.'" Whitaker, *Disputation on Holy Scripture*, 36–37. This comment is from the Cambridge divine William Whitaker, whose book mentioned above was considered one of the seminal Protestant works on biblical authority. Throughout his book, Whitaker constantly affirmed his belief in an errorless text. Further, he believed that his view replicated that of Augustine precisely. His rationale was much the same as the fathers—since the Holy Spirit was the author of Scripture, it necessarily must be perfect. He wrote concerning the transmission process: "They wrote as they were moved by the Holy Ghost, as Peter tells us, 2 Pet 1:21. And all Scripture is inspired of God, as Paul expressly writes, 2 Tim 3:16. Whereas, therefore, no one may say that any infirmity could befall the Holy Spirit, it follows that the sacred writers could not be deceived or err in any respect. Here, then, it becomes us to be so scrupulous as not to allow that any such slip can be found in Scripture." Whitaker, *Disputation*, 36–38.

witnesses and ministers of the Word, delivered to the fathers; it seemed good to me also, having been urged thereto by true brethren, and having learned from the beginning, to set before you the books included in the Canon, and handed down and accredited as Divine.... These are fountains of salvation, that they who thirst may be satisfied with the living words they contain. In these alone is proclaimed the doctrine of godliness. Let no man add to these, neither let him take ought from these.[5]

Though he arranged the books in a slightly different configuration than is common today, (for instance by including 1 and 2 Samuel with the books of Kings), the rendering is identical, with the single omission of the book of Esther. It is likely that Esther was subsumed within the book of Ezra as was the case with Nehemiah.

Furthermore, one finds equal precision regarding the New Testament. Athanasius assigned the book of Hebrews to Pauline authorship, which is disputed. Nonetheless, he classified the New Testament books exactly as they appear today, carefully differentiating between the inspired collection and the apocryphal books, which he deemed helpful but not divinely inspired.[6] Thus it seems safe to conclude that the early church held the 66 canonical books of Scripture in the highest esteem, viewing them as the product of divine authorship and wielding absolute authority, whether the divine voice addressed matters of facts or faith—down to the exact words.[7]

Much the same may be said about the Reformation church. In a very real sense, the medieval church lost the concept of biblical authority, transferring that leadership to the organized church and its hierarchy of clerical leaders. The Reformers believed that the church had failed in its custodial mission as keepers of the book. In becoming corrupt, it had abnegated the right to govern. A new authority was needed. Their rallying cries reveal much about their perspective: *sola Scriptura* and *sola fide*—Scripture alone and faith alone.

5. Schaff and Wace, *Nicene and Post-Nicene Fathers*, 4:551–52.

6. Ibid.

7. Origen, one of the key fathers of the Alexandrian church, wrote, "... we must, in order to establish the positions we have laid down, adduce the testimony of Holy Scripture. And that this testimony may produce a sure and unhesitating belief ... it seems necessary to show, in the first place, that the Scriptures themselves are divine, i.e., were inspired by the Spirit of God. We shall therefore with all possible brevity draw forth from the Holy Scriptures themselves, such evidence on this point as may produce upon us a suitable impression." Roberts and Donaldson, *Ante-Nicene Fathers*, 4:349.

The Reformers reclaimed the concept of biblical authority. The Scripture was the final arbiter of all matters, they insisted. One influential reformer, William Whitaker, wrote a significant treatise on the Bible entitled, *A Disputation on Holy Scripture*. In this book, Whitaker constantly affirmed the divine character of the Bible, endorsing its inspired status. Such a status, he argued, rendered Scripture completely exempt from all error. His conviction on this point might be most clearly observed in a theological confrontation with Melchior Canus. In seeking to explain divergent readings in the text, Canus suggested that the early church martyr Stephen had erred as recorded in Acts 7. Whitaker's commitment to biblical inerrancy would not allow him to accept such a remedy. In refutation of this idea, Whitaker wrote:

> Stephen, therefore, could no more have mistaken than Luke, because the Holy Ghost was the same in Luke and in Stephen, and had no less force in the one than in the other. . . . Therefore, we must maintain in tact the authority of Scripture in such a sense as not to allow that anything is therein delivered otherwise than the most perfect truth required.[8]

Because the Holy Spirit functioned as the clandestine composer of the Bible, using the various human writers as his amanuensis, Scripture could not possibly contain a mistake regarding anything. In fact, to suggest such a thing was tantamount to impugning God's character as a conveyor of falsehood. Whitaker and other Reformers would brook no such conclusion. Even in apparent discrepancy, the Bible could always be harmonized because God would never contradict himself, they urged.[9]

8. Whitaker, *Disputation on Holy Scripture*, 38.

9. Orthodox theologians diligently sought to silence critics who accused the Bible of internal contradictions, thus seriously eroding the doctrine of inerrancy. One such dispute pertained to the hour of Christ's crucifixion. Regarding this hour, the gospel of Mark and that of John appeared to have a serious discrepancy between them. According to the gospel of Mark, Jesus was already crucified by "the third hour," but John's gospel stated that Pilate was still considering his best option at about "the sixth hour" (Mark 15:25 and John 19:14). The manner in which theologian William Lee sought to harmonize these two accounts is typical. Lee stated, "It has been reserved for modern times to suggest a solution which has been almost universally accepted, and which removes every shade of difficulty from the case. . . . The explanation for this apparent discordance in time . . . is, that S. John has given the hour according to the Roman calculation of time, which counted as we do, from midnight; while S. Mark adheres to the Jewish custom of counting from sunrise." Lee, *Inspiration of Holy Scripture*, 351–2. So, according to Lee's harmony the two accounts correspond perfectly. Pilate was in fact considering his op-

Following the Reformation, this unwavering confidence in the fidelity of the Scripture was sustained in Europe for about 200 years and in America until the close of the nineteenth century.[10] In his classic text, *Evidences of the Authenticity, Inspiration, and Canonical Authority of the Holy Scriptures,* Archibald Alexander, the first professor at Princeton Seminary, offered a definition of inspiration that is representative of the traditional orthodoxy of the time. Alexander wrote:

> The true definition of inspiration, then, is SUCH A DIVINE INFLUENCE UPON THE MINDS OF THE SACRED WRITERS AS RENDERED THEM EXEMPT FROM ERROR, BOTH IN REGARD TO THE IDEAS AND THE WORDS. This is properly called PLENARY inspiration. Nothing can be conceived more satisfactory. Certainty, infallible certainty, is the most that can be desired in any narrative; and if we have this in the sacred Scriptures, there is nothing more to be wished in regard to this matter.[11]

Employing capital letters, Alexander seemed bent upon making his position unmistakably clear. He believed that the sacred penmen operated under the direction of the Holy Spirit which rendered them incapable of mistake. This exemption from error applied both to the thoughts and ideas as well as to the actual words employed by them. Thus it is clear that Alexander considered the biblical product infallible, without defect, completely reliable in every respect.[12] Though the nineteenth- and twentieth-

tions at the sixth hour or about 6 o'clock in the morning, before deciding to crucify Christ at Mark's third hour or about 9 o'clock in the morning. Conservative theologians believed that Scripture was consistent and accurate in every detail.

10. During the fractious controversies over the doctrine of Scripture in the nineteenth century, theological liberals regularly conceded that inerrancy represented the traditional orthodox opinion of the church. George Ladd was one such liberal who confessed, "The only attempt which any large section of the Christian Church has ever made, rigidly to formulate the doctrine of Sacred Scripture, resulted in what we have called the post-Reformation dogma. This dogma was dominant in the Protestant, and especially in the Reformed churches, from about the year 1600 AD until the middle of the eighteenth century. . . . The dogma with a sure instinct seemed to feel that its life in the future depended upon its ability to defend successfully the . . . infallibility of Sacred Scripture." Ladd, *Doctrine of Sacred Scripture,* 1:9.

11. Alexander, *Evidences of Authenticity,* 230.

12. Alexander's influential colleague at Princeton, Charles Hodge, endorsed precisely the same doctrine, writing, "The guidance of the Spirit extended to the words no less than to the thoughts of the sacred writers . . . the guidance of the Spirit extended to the words employed. . . . To deny, in such cases, the control of the Spirit over the words of the sacred writers, is to deny inspiration altogether. . . . The view, therefore, everywhere pre-

century debates over the doctrine of Scripture recast biblical orthodoxy in many mainline denominations, millions of conservative Protestants continue to endorse the doctrine of biblical inerrancy until this very day. But why would anyone believe such a thing?

In assessing this question, a number of elements factor into the equation. Some who take the comments of Scripture seriously assert that the internal testimony of the Bible conclusively indicates that it is of divine origin. For others who find these ancient writings less than persuasive, the truth claims of Scripture can be tested against matters of history and geography that the Bible describes.

Of course, the fact that the Bible is historically and geographically accurate would not prove it is of divine origin. But if it is accurate, it would enhance the Bible's reputation as a conveyor of reliable secular information. Since I suspect many people believe the Bible is nothing more than a collection of myths and legends, accuracy in such matters would elevate its status and certainly be consistent with a high view of inspiration.

Finally, there is fulfilled prophecy. Since it is humanly impossible to forecast the future with specificity, the fact that Scripture consistently does so with startling precision seems to indicate that it is a unique composition—one deserving attention. Liberal theologians have done their best to transform prophecy into history through various dating techniques—they understand the explosive implications of a book that can predict the future. However, such tactics are futile against many prophecies, particularly those that speak to and about Christ. Indeed this last piece of evidence may leave even the most skeptical perplexed.

ITS INTERNAL TESTIMONY

Theologians across time and space have appealed to many of the same internal proofs to argue that Scripture is notably different from any and all other literature. Indeed, the development of the canon itself testifies to this fact, since only books deemed "God-breathed" were admitted. This section briefly outlines some of the major evidences employed for asserting the divine origin of the Bible.

---

sented in the New Testament of the inspiration of the ancient prophets, supposes them to be under the guidance of the Holy Spirit in the words they employ." C. Hodge, review of *Inspiration of Holy Scripture*, 675–7. Hodge stated the same premise more succinctly in his *Systematic Theology* where he noted, "The thoughts are in the words, the two are inseparable." C. Hodge, *Systematic Theology*, 1:164.

Conservatives have consistently marshaled the voice of two critical texts to argue their point: 2 Timothy 3:16 and 2 Peter 1:21.[13] The former passage reads "All Scripture is God-breathed and is useful for teaching, rebuking, correcting, and training in righteousness." The function of the adjective "God-breathed" is the main point for consideration. It could be translated in one of two ways: in either an attributive or predicate sense.

If it were functioning attributively the text would read, "All God-breathed Scripture is profitable." The adjective attributes a quality to the noun "Scripture," making it sound as though some Scripture is inspired and some is not. In an age of reason, this was particularly appealing to theological liberals who increasingly became uncomfortable with endorsing the "facts" of the Bible as infallible. However, if the predicate use of the adjective is preferred, the text reads, "All Scripture is God-breathed," meaning that whatever may properly be called Scripture is a divine product. Of course this referred only to the canonical books. Grammatically, the predicate sense is preferable. If the adjective functioned in the attributive sense, one would expect it to either precede the noun "Scripture" or

13. Rev. Joseph Lampe, one of the members of the Prosecuting Committee in the well known heresy case of Charles Briggs, quoted 2 Tim 3:16 as evidence for the verbal inspiration and error free quality of the Bible. He also turned to 2 Pet 1:21 to buttress this contention, demonstrating that the Holy Spirit himself had authored the text, proving that no error could possibly invade the original "God-breathed" manuscript. Lampe asserted that history firmly sustained the inerrant position and that it replicated the opinion of the New Testament Church as well as that of the great Reformers. All of the fathers and the Reformers belonged in the inerrant category, Lampe stated. He noted, "It is preposterous at this late day to advance the claim that insisting on the truthfulness of the Bible is tantamount to setting up a new test of orthodoxy. The Church has never believed anything else. Especially is this true of the Presbyterian Church. It will not be possible to point to a single representative Presbyterian divine, from the Westminster period down, and especially among American Presbyterians, who has taught the doctrine of the errancy of Scripture. All sides, parties, and schools in our Church have been agreed in affirming the inerrancy of the Word of God. Green, Alexander, and C. Hodge cordially unite with Richards and Barnes in subscribing to the statement of Dr. Henry B. Smith that inspiration extends to both thoughts and words and gives us 'truth without error' in the Bible. Our Church has always held that, when we have determined the exact historic-grammatical meaning of a statement in the Bible, we have then the absolute truthfulness of that statement certified to us by the Spirit of God." Satta, *Sacred Text*, 89. Indeed, Lampe was heartily supported in his assessment. The General Assembly of the Presbyterian Church of America sided with him overwhelmingly against Briggs, who they defrocked from the Presbyterian Church for heresy. The General Assembly endorsed biblical inerrancy as essential orthodoxy. For a more detailed account of the trial see Satta, *Sacred Text*, 75–96.

have the definite article. In the original Greek neither is the case. So the best rendering of the passage is, "All Scripture is God-breathed."[14]

The second passage for consideration is 2 Peter 1:21 which reads, "For prophecy never had its origin in the will of man, but men spoke from God as they were carried along by the Holy Spirit." One immediately notes the strong force of the adversative "but," ruling out human origination. The negative is emphatic, stating the production was *not* by the will of man *but* by the Holy Spirit. The superintending guidance of the Holy Spirit is reflected by the participle rendered: "were carried along." This text attributes composition to the Holy Spirit while expressly denying human origin. In light of these two passages and their insistence on the divine origin of Scripture, it is easy to forgive members of the ancient church for endorsing the mechanical dictation theory.[15]

The theological elite also frequently appealed to the testimony of Jesus Christ to support their position. Jesus, as portrayed by the gospel historians, consistently confirmed the literal, historical reliability of the Old Testament. Indeed, in Matthew 5:17–18, Jesus offered commentary on the sacrosanct character of Scripture stating, "Do not think that I am come to abolish the law or the prophets, I have not come to abolish them but to fulfill them. I tell you the truth, until heaven and earth disappear, not the smallest letter, not the least stroke of a pen, will by any means disappear from the law until all be fulfilled." It would have been difficult for Jesus to state his respect for the words of the Scripture with greater emphasis.

Furthermore, Jesus affirmed the Mosaic authorship of the Pentateuch, affirming its teaching at every level (Matt 19:8; Mark 7:10; 10:3; Luke 5:14). He believed the predictive words of the prophet Daniel (Mark 13:14) and viewed the sojourn by the Queen of Sheba to admire Solomon's riches

---

14. In his definitive Greek grammar, A.T. Robertson notes that while it is remotely possible for the adjective in 2 Tim 3:16 to function attributively, it is rare for it to do so. He observes, "When the article is used before the adjective, it is of course, attributive. . . ." He then goes on to state that it is possible for the adjective to retain its attributive quality without the article, if it appears directly before the noun. But the adjective in 2 Tim 3:16 appears after the noun and without the article, making the predicate function highly likely. Robertson, *Grammar of the Greek New Testament*, 656.

15. The mechanical theory maintained that the Holy Spirit took absolute control of the human writers in such a way that they served merely as tools without providing any human element whatsoever. This notion fell from favor as textual critics identified the presence of human personality in the various books of the Bible. For instance, Paul had a particular style as did John, Luke, Matthew, Mark, etc.

as historically precise. Jesus even accredited the book of Jonah as being reliable in every detail, including Jonah's consumption by the great fish and the subsequent revival in Nineveh (Matt 12:40–41). At no point in the gospel narratives does Jesus question the accuracy or historical legitimacy of any first covenant account.

Such appeals to the internal voice of Scripture proved compelling to ancient theologians, scholars, and church leaders, yet they may exert no force upon the present reader. The purpose of this brief excursus is informative not persuasive. We now know what the church believed about the Bible through much of its history, and, to a degree, why they believed it. Indeed, the Scripture offers direct testimony about itself as the product of divine origination. But is there anything less biased and more concrete that might be called upon as a witness in support? An innocent man falsely accused of a crime will plead not guilty. His family members and close friends will likely believe him. But his voice alone will probably not convince an impartial jury; they want proof. His lawyer will introduce other corroborating evidence. Is there any other circumstantial evidence to substantiate Scripture's testimony that it is a special composition?

In order to assess Scripture's claim objectively, one must examine its contents regarding things that can actually be tested. Is its character one of integrity and truthfulness or one of error? I suspect that most people think that such an examination would prove an embarrassment to the Bible, believing that it is filled with verifiable errors and inaccuracies of many kinds. This assumption is incorrect. In fact, the Scripture is amazingly precise in matters related to real history and actual geography. One might object that these issues are relatively mundane. Quite so, but if Scripture precisely articulates such secular matters, perhaps it is also trustworthy regarding things which are beyond our ability to examine.

What was generally assumed in the ancient and Reformation church, based upon the internal witness of the Bible, came under great scrutiny and criticism in America in the nineteenth century. Increasingly, Protestant leaders, under duress from the emerging science of geology, Darwinism, textual criticism, and theological liberalism, were urged to abandon the doctrine of biblical inerrancy. The debate incited an impressive defense of Scripture by orthodox leaders, pointing out the startling precision with which Scripture spoke. Orthodox leaders stood resolutely in favor of biblical inerrancy. The comments of G. Frederick Wright, professor at Oberlin Theological Seminary, while defending the Princeton Seminary faculty and their commitment to inerrancy, are characteristic:

> For they and the scholars agreeing with them are emboldened to take this position both by the claims of the sacred writers themselves and by the futility of all the efforts during these eighteen hundred years to convict the Scriptures of any error. So universally have these efforts at criticism failed, that the presumption is exceedingly strong that the original writers did not make any mistakes.[16]

HISTORICAL AND GEOGRAPHICAL PRECISION

Upon a judicious sifting of the biblical record, one discovers a consistent testimony of truth and accuracy in matters that can be tested. The Scripture factually depicts the people, places, customs, kingdoms, wars, and other events of the ancient world, including even minor details and incidentals, with integrity.[17] Of course, this fact alone does not prove that the Bible is a divine composition, but it does indicate that it is consistent with such an idea.

Scripture is a large document containing thousands of historical and geographical details.[18] This analysis will assess just a few points of

16. Wright, "Dr. Briggs, 'Wither,'" 138.

17. Merrill Unger offers a brief synopsis of the developing archaeological support that corroborates many aspects of Old Testament history. "One can only imagine the fervor aroused among serious students of the Bible by illuminating discoveries in Biblical lands especially from about 1800 to the present. . . . With the decipherment of the Rosetta Stone, which unlocked Egyptian hieroglyphics, and the decipherment of the Behistun inscription, which furnished the key to Assyrian-Babylonian cuneiform, a vast mass of material bearing on the Old Testament was released. The discovery of the Moabite Stone in 1868 created a veritable sensation because of its close connection with Old Testament history and excited widespread interest in Palestinian excavations. However, many of the most notable discoveries affecting the Bible and particularly the Old Testament were not made until approximately the last half century. Such finds as the Code of Hammurabi (1901), the Elephantine Papyri (1903), the Hittite Monuments . . . (1906), the tomb of Tutankhamun (1922), the Sarcophagus of Ahiram of Byblus (1923), the Ras Shamra texts (1929–1937), the Mari Letters and the Lachish Ostraca (1935–1938), and the Dead Sea Scrolls (1947) are famous in large measure because of their close connection with the literature and the history of the Old Testament." Unger, *Archaeology and the Old Testament*, 10.

18. Archaeological evidence in support of the Scripture's claims and depictions is impressive. The few instances I cite in the narrative could be multiplied hundreds of times. Donald Wiseman suggests that concerning the geography of Bible lands, nearly 25,000 sites have been located and confirmed via archaeology. Wiseman, "Archaeological Confirmation," 301–2. Wiseman notes, "Many parallels between the predominantly

agreement between Scripture and secular knowledge. This harmony is particularly impressive because it indicates first-hand knowledge on the part of the biblical writers as well as great attention to detail. Of course the

Hurrian (Horite) tablets of Nuzi have been described by Gordon and Speiser. Thus the relation of Eliezer to Abraham, as adoptee to a childless couple who yields his right to the real heir, is now explained (Gen 15:2–4), as is the action of Sarah in providing Hagar for her husband. Moreover, Abraham may have felt able to break with contemporary custom in driving Hagar away only when given a special assurance by God to do so (Gen 21:12). . . . It was common practice for a man to work for his bride, as did Jacob among the Aramaean tribe of Laban. Oral blessing having legal force, and Levirate marriage, the right of a daughter to inherit property . . . are other customs found at this time. The force of these parallels is all the stronger since the Alalakh texts show that throughout the Upper Euphrates region in the early second millennium there was an essentially homogenous culture with a Sumerian basis but a mixed Amorite-Hurrian development. The Nuzi texts reflect a later stage in this culture. It must be continually remembered that the Old Testament implies, as do these documents, a mixed population in Palestine including Hittites whose early infiltration there is now indicated by the Alalakh texts. M.R. Lehman has shown how applicable the Hittite laws are to the negotiations by Abraham for the cave of Machpelah (Gen 23). The distinctive features of legal contracts . . . ; the patriarch's concern over obtaining a title to the land free from feudal obligations; . . . are all characteristic of these Hittite business documents. As Dr. Lehman has rightly emphasized, 'We have thus found that Genesis 23 is permeated with the knowledge of intricate subtleties of Hittite laws and customs correctly corresponding to the time of Abraham and fitting in with the Hittite features of the Biblical account. . . . Our study again confirms the authenticity of the "background material" of the Old Testament . . . 'This increase in knowledge of the patriarchal age from the texts, combined with the archaeological evidence, has led scholars of many shades of religious opinion to affirm the "historical" nature of the patriarchal narratives.' . . . Professor H.H. Rowley claims that 'it is not because scholars of today begin with more conservative presuppositions than their predecessors that they have a much greater respect for the Patriarchal stories than was formerly common, but because the evidence warrants it.'" Ibid., 304–5.

Regarding the New Testament, Norman Geisler notes that "there is specific confirmation of specific facts of New Testament history from archaeology. . . . There are literally hundreds of archaeological finds that support specific persons, events, and facts presented in Luke–Acts, including many which were once thought to be incorrect. Especially noteworthy is Luke's correct usages of official titles. He calls the rulers of Thessalonica 'politarchs,' Gallio the 'Proconsul of Achaea,' the one in Ephesus a 'Temple Warden,' the governor of Cyprus a 'proconsul,' and the chief official in Malta 'the first man of the island,' a title confirmed in Greek and Latin inscriptions. Likewise, Luke is known to be correct in chronological references. His reference to 'Lysanius the tetrarch of Abilene' at the time John the Baptist began his ministry (A.D. 27), once thought to be incorrect, is now known by Greek inscriptions to be correct. Lysanius was tetrarch between A.D. 14 and 29. Other chronological references are known to be correct including those to Caesar, Herod, and even Gallio (Acts 18:12–17)." Geisler, *Christian Apologetics*, 325–6. Furthermore, many places named in the Gospels have received independent verification by archaeology, such as the Pool of Siloam (John 9:7–11) and the "Judgment Seat" near Corinth mentioned in 2 Cor 5:10. Ibid.

reader is encouraged to investigate these and other claims of the Bible.[19] Historical and geographic details will be examined from the prophet Daniel and the book of Acts.

It is widely agreed by secular and sacred historians that the Babylonian exile of which Scripture speaks in detail (in Kings, Chronicles, and the prophets) is an actual historical fact; it really happened. Just as secular historians agree that the Jews suffered enslavement at the hands of the Egyptians for 400 years, so they also concede that the Jews spent roughly 70 years in exile at Babylon.[20]

19. For further reading on this issue I recommend the following works: Merrill F. Unger, *Archaeology and the Old Testament*, and Sherwin-White, *Roman Society and Roman Law in the New Testament*.

20. "Perhaps the most unanswerable bit of testimony that part of Israel (the tribe of Levi at least) resided in Egypt for a long time is the surprising number of Egyptian personal names in the Levitical genealogies. For example: Moses, Assir, Pashhur, Hophni, Phinehas, Merari, and Puti-el in its first element are all 'unquestionably Egyptian.'... There are moreover, a great many correct local and antiquarian details in the Egyptian narratives in Genesis and Exodus which, like the general fact of the sojourn of Jacob's twelve sons and their posterity in the land of the Nile, would be inexplicable as later inventions. The story of Joseph, which is one of the finest and most dramatic stories in all literature, furnishes an example. In the moving narrative there are 'many bits of Egyptian coloring . . . which have been fully illustrated by Egyptological discoveries.' When the writer, for instance, has the occasion to mention the titles of Egyptian officials, 'he employs the correct title in use and exactly as it was used at the period referred to, and, where there is no Hebrew equivalent, he simply adopts the Egyptian word and transliterates it into Hebrew.' The titles of 'chief of the butlers' and 'chief of the bakers' (Gen 40:2) are those of palace officials mentioned in Egyptian documents. When Potiphar made Joseph 'overseer of his house' (Gen 39:4), the title employed in the narrative is a direct translation of an official position in the houses of Egyptian nobility. Moreover Pharaoh gave Joseph an office with a similar title in the administration of the realm (Gen 41:40), which corresponds exactly to the office of prime minister or vizier of Egypt, who was the chief administrator in the country, second in power to the Pharaoh himself. In Egypt there was also an office of 'superintendent of the granaries.' This was of special significance since the stability of the country lay in its grain, and Joseph may have exercised this function in view of the approaching famine, in addition to his duties as prime minister. The Pharaoh's gifts to Joseph upon the latter's induction into office would be quite in accord with Egyptian custom: 'And Pharaoh took off his signet ring from his hand, and put it upon Joseph's hand, and arrayed him in vestures of fine linen, and put a gold chain around his neck; and made him ride in the second chariot which he had; and they cried before him, Bow the knee' (Gen 41:42–43). Other striking instances of authentic local color in the story of Joseph are numerous. There is, for example, ample evidence of famines in Egypt (cf. Gen 41). At least two Egyptian officials, giving a synopsis of their good deeds on the walls of their tombs, list dispensing food to the needy 'in each year of want.' One inscription written about 100 B.C. actually tells of a seven-year famine in the days of Pharaoh Zoser of the Third Dynasty (c. 2700 B.C.)." Unger, *Archaeology and the Old Testament*, 130–3.

There was a time when some liberal theologians argued that this was all mythical nonsense. The names seemed so foreign that they could hardly believe that they portrayed real people and authentic civilizations. For instance, this was the case regarding the Babylonian monarch who led the overthrow of Jerusalem, Nebuchadnezzar. Admittedly, that name is a mouthful. But was he an actual historical figure? Yes! Thanks to the hard work of archaeologists, evidence was uncovered confirming the testimony of the Bible. In excavating the area of ancient Babylon, bricks were unearthed that offered conclusive testimony. The bricks had writing etched upon them and each presented the same message. The inscription on each one read "Nebuchadnezzar, son of Nabopolassar."[21] The Bible's testimony was confirmed via archaeology.

Another Babylonian king provides additional support to the biblical record. Daniel 5:30 records the death of Belshazzar the king of the Chaldeans on the night the Medo-Persians invaded and overthrew Babylon (another historically verified event). Invading forces under the command of Cyrus decimated Babylon and killed the king. However, the name Belshazzar was not attested to by any other source for a long time. Secular historians argued that the biblical record was in error because according to other ancient sources, Nabonidus was the final king in Babylon. Since no mention of Belshazzar occurred outside the Bible, it was generally assumed the Bible was wrong. The extra-biblical accounts contended that Nabonidus, hearing of the invasion, went to Babylon to oppose the invaders, that he was defeated and later shown clemency at the hands of Cyrus, who sent him to Carmania, where he later died.

This appeared to refute the historical reliability of Scripture. However, an important discovery by Rawlinson in 1854 removed the apparent discrepancy. Theologian William Lee comments on this:

> A number of clay cylinders have been lately disinterred in the ruins of Um-Qeer (the ancient Ur of the Chaldees), two of which contain a memorial of the works executed by Nabonidus (the last king of Babylon) in Southern Chaldaea. The most important fact that they disclose is, that the eldest son of Nabonidus was named Bel-shar-ezzar, and that he was admitted by his father to share in the government. This name is undoubtedly the Belshazzar . . . of Daniel, and thus furnishes us with a key to the explanation of that great historical problem which has hitherto defied solution. We can

21. Robinson, "Rawlinson's Historical Evidences," 510–1.

now understand how Belshazzar, as joint king with his father, may have been governor of Babylon, when the city was attacked by the combined forces of the Medes and Persians, and may have perished in the assault that followed. . . . By the discovery, indeed, of the name of Bel-shar-ezzar, as appertaining to the son of Nabonidus, we are, for the first time, enabled to reconcile . . . history with the inspired record of Daniel. [22]

In both these cases, the accuracy of the Bible was confirmed by additional secular input. While early critics ridiculed the testimony of Scripture, when more facts appeared the biblical account was vindicated.

Another incidental statement found in Daniel indicates the meticulous care given to apparently minor details. On the night of the Persian overthrow, the Babylonians were reveling, drinking from vessels taken from the Jewish Temple. Mysteriously, a hand appeared out of nowhere and wrote an arcane message on the wall. The people were terrified. Daniel

---

22. Lee, *Inspiration*, 349. The details of the New Testament are defended as equally precise. In explaining an alleged historical blunder in Luke, William Lee explained, "S. Luke in the thirteenth chapter gives the title of Proconsul to the Governor of Cypress. In this division, however, of the Roman Empire by Augustus, this island had been reserved for his own jurisdiction: and consequently its Governor must have borne the rank Procurator;—that of Proconsul being appropriated to those who ruled the provinces which the Emperor had ceded to the Senate. The title here assigned by S. Luke to Sergius Paulus had for a long time perplexed commentators; who knew not how to reconcile the statement of the sacred historian with the assumed facts of the case. Some coins, however, were found bearing the effigy of the Emperor Claudius; and in the centre of the reverse occurs the word Cypress, while the surrounding legend gives the title in question of Proconsul to an individual who must have been the immediate successor or predecessor of Sergius Paulus. In addition to this evidence, a passage has been pointed out in the writings of Dio Cassius who mentions that Augustus, subsequently to his original settlement, had changed Cyprus and Gallia Narbonensis into Senatorial Provinces; the historian adding, as if with the design of establishing S. Luke's accuracy, 'And so it came to pass, that Proconsuls began to be sent to these nations also.'" Ibid., 363–4.

And Gleason Archer concurs with Lee on Belshazzar, noting, "During the last century, it was customary for late-date advocates to assume that the mention of Belshazzar was completely unhistorical since extrabiblical historical sources refer to Nabonidus as the final king of the Babylonian Empire. After the discovery of oath-tablets in Neo-Babylonian cuneiform dating from the twelfth year of Nabonidus (543 B.C.) and associating Belshazzar, his son, with him on an equal footing . . . it became startlingly apparent that the writer of Daniel was much more accurately informed about the history of the 540s in Babylon than Herodotus was in 450 B.C. Thus the argument based on the silence of extrabiblical Greek sources concerning Belshazzar not only collapsed but turned out to be a powerful argument in favor of the sixth-century date for the writing of the book." Archer, "Daniel," 7:15–16.

was hailed to come and interpret the writing. In Daniel 5:16 there is a record of what Belshazzar said to him when he arrived: "Now I have heard that you are able to give interpretations and to solve difficult problems. If you can read this writing and tell me what it means, you will be clothed in purple and have a gold chain placed around your neck, and *you will be made the third highest ruler in the kingdom*" [italics mine].

What is so significant about the final phrase of his offer? Well, the reader might have puzzled that Daniel was offered third place in the kingdom rather than second place. The book of Daniel depicts Belshazzar as the king and makes no mention of Nabonidus. But the text faithfully recorded what Belshazzar most likely really did say. If Belshazzar was a co-regent with his father, as now seems probable, then his offer to make Daniel the "third ruler" sounds incredibly authentic. The text makes no commentary on the details of this desperate offer. It simply records it. Only looking back, informed from a variety of sacred and secular sources, does it make complete sense. Such scrupulous care to accurately represent a minor historical detail is stunning.

Now the fact that the Bible represents historical people, places, and events with exactness does not prove it is divine. But it does at least suggest that it should be catalogued in the history section rather than among works of mythology.[23] These three brief illustrations might only be a cu-

---

23. Not only is the antagonism between Judah and Babylon historically verified, but that which existed between Judah's King Hezekiah and the Assyrians as well. Unger notes, "The Assyrian king in 701 B.C. launched his great western campaign to punish Hezekiah and other recalcitrants and bring them back under the Assyrian yoke. This important undertaking is not only graphically described in the Bible but is also recorded in the annals of Sennacherib which were recorded on clay cylinders or prisms. The final edition of these annals is found on the so-called Taylor prism of the British Museum and a copy on a prism in the Oriental Institute of the University of Chicago. In detail Sennacherib describes his third campaign, which was directed against Syria-Palestine and embraced the siege of Jerusalem. . . . Sennacherib makes a lengthy reference to his attack on Hezekiah's realm: 'As for Hezekiah, the Jew, who did not submit to my yoke, 46 of his strong walled cities, as well as the small cities in their neighborhood, which were without number,—by escalade and by bringing up siege engines, by attacking and storming on foot, by mines, tunnels, and breaches; I besieged and took. 200,150 people, great and small, male and female, horses, mules, asses, camels, cattle, and sheep, without number I brought away from them and counted as spoil. Himself, like a caged bird, I shut up in Jerusalem, his royal city. . . . I added to the former tribute, and laid upon him as their yearly payment, a tax in the form of gifts for my majesty. As for Hezekiah, the terrifying splendor of my majesty overcame him and the Urbi [Arabs] and his mercenary [picked] troops which he had brought in to defend Jerusalem, his royal city, deserted him. In addition to 30 talents of gold and 800 talents of silver, there were gems, antimony, jewels, large sandu-stones, couches of

riosity if not for the fact that they are indicative of the historical probity one encounters throughout the Scripture as far as one can examine. Nor is it just history that is incisively related but the geography of the ancient world is mapped out in Scripture with the care of an expert topographer. This first-hand discovery led one theological liberal to reassess his view of the Bible.[24]

---

ivory, house chairs of ivory, elephant's hide, ivory, maple, boxwood, all kinds of valuable treasures, as well as his daughters, his harem, his male and female musicians, which he had them bring after me to Nineveh, my royal city. To pay tribute and to accept servitude he dispatched his messengers.' Seemingly the account of Sennacherib's western campaign recorded in the Taylor prism is the same as that described in II Kings 18:13—19:37; II Chronicles 32:1-12 and Isaiah 36:1—37:38. A great deal of light is shed on the biblical narrative by the monuments and there are numerous striking points of agreement, proving that the campaign of 701 B.C. is the one described in the Bible." Unger, *Archaeology*, 267–68. The violent demise of Sennacherib as described in the Scripture is corroborated precisely by Assyrian documents. Unger states, "Sennacherib was a fiendishly cruel and inhuman ruler, guilty of impaling and flaying his foes alive and other incredible atrocities. He died as he lived—a victim of violence and treachery. The Bible tells us he met his end at Nineveh at the hands of his own sons. 'And it came to pass, that as he was worshipping in the house of Nishroch his god, that Adrammelech [Assyrian Adadmilki] and Sharezar [Shar-usur] his sons smote him with the sword: they escaped into the land of Ararat. And Esarhaddon his son reigned in his stead' (Isa 37:38; cf. II Kings 19:37). Esarhaddon (681–668 B.C.), Sennacherib's son and successor, relates this very event in an inscription: 'In the month of Nisanu, on a favorable day. . . . I made my joyful entrance into the royal palace, the awesome place wherein abides the fate of kings. A firm determination fell upon my brothers. They forsook the gods and turned to their deeds of violence, plotting evil. . . . To gain the kingship they slew Sennacherib their father.'" Ibid., 269–70.

24. I will restrict my comments in the narrative to the case of Sir William Ramsey. However, the geographical accuracy of the Scripture was and is a topic of great interest to biblical scholars. One writer assessing the locale of Hebron in relation to Sodom argued that the Pentateuch was vindicated in its demographic depiction: "From the height which overlooks Hebron, where Abraham stood . . . the observer at the present day has an extensive view spread out before him towards the Dead Sea. The hills of Moab, sloping down towards that sea to the east, and a part of Idumea, are all in sight. A cloud of smoke rising from the plain would be visible to a person at Hebron now, and could have been, therefore, to Abraham, as he looked towards Sodom on the morning after its destruction by Jehovah." "Geographical Accuracy of the Bible," 452. Two well known conservative scholars of the nineteenth century, A.A. Hodge and Benjamin Warfield also pointed out the impressive geographical reporting of the Scripture, writing: "Between forty and fifty names of countries can be counted in the New Testament pages; every one is accurately named and placed. About the same number of foreign cities are named, and all equally accurately. Still more to the purpose, thirty-six Syrian and Palestinian towns are named, the great majority of which have been identified . . . this unvarying accuracy of statement is certainly consistent with the strictest doctrine of inspiration." A.A. Hodge and Warfield, "Inspiration," 252.

Sir William Ramsey, theological liberal, archaeologist, and explorer, traveled to Asia Minor to conduct work. As most liberals of the late nineteenth century, Ramsey viewed Scripture as little more than a fairy tale. He hardly expected it to function as a reliable conveyor of concrete factual information about the topography of the region. However, as no reliable charts and maps of the area existed, he turned to the book of Acts, by default, to see if it might offer a little help to him in his travels.

What Ramsey discovered changed his view of the Bible entirely. When put to the test, Ramsey found that the course charted by the apostle Paul concerning his first missionary journey (Acts chapters 13–14) accurately reflected the terrain of Asia Minor. Ramsey traced the trip as described by the biblical writer, Luke, and found that Paul's accounting made complete sense. Paul reported that he left Antioch and traveled to Selucia, and that is exactly the course one would take in order to sail to the island of Cyprus as Selucia was a coastal village just south of Antioch. According to the text, they sailed from Selucia and landed at Salamis. Salamis is located on the eastern shore of Cyprus, just as is described.

Furthermore, the account states that they then traversed the island, concluding their mission at Paphos. Indeed, Paphos is a coastal village on the far western shore of Cyprus. From there they sailed to Perga in the region of Pamphilia, and this is directly North West of Paphos. Perga, like Selucia, Salamis, and Paphos, is in point of fact a coastal port. The biblical account declares that Paul and Barnabas then traveled to Pisidian Antioch which is directly north of Perga. And from there they journeyed to Iconium to offer witness. It harmonized perfectly.

However, Ramsey thought he had detected an error on the part of Luke regarding a statement made in chapter 14. Here the Bible states that Paul and Barnabas left Iconium and traveled to a different region, the Lycaonian cities of Derbe and Lystra. These two towns are just south of Iconium. But Ramsey was convinced that all three locales; Iconium, Derbe, and Lystra were part of Lycaonia. Thus he concluded that Luke was simply wrong, stating that they entered a different region. However, upon closer inspection he found that the mistake was his own. At the time of Luke's record, Iconium was actually in Phrygia not Lycaonia as Ramsey had believed. Ramsey was greatly impressed that Luke had made such a discriminating observation of such a minor detail. His assessment of the record afforded by Luke in Acts was that it could withstand the most stringent scrutiny.[25]

Luke's precision so captivated Ramsey that he eventually traced all of Paul's journeys throughout the Roman Empire, writing an influential volume entitled, *Paul the Traveller and Roman Citizen*. Ramsey's surprising conclusion based upon his first-hand encounter with the text and the topography of Asia Minor led him to the conviction that Scripture is thoroughly reliable.[26] Historical accuracy and geographic precision are not the only factors consistent with Scripture's claim. There is another characteristic that, to my mind, sets the Bible apart from any other source—prophecy.

FULFILLED PROPHECY

Consider the shock and amazement if archaeologists discovered a document dated in the year 1700 that contained the following inscription, "On January 1, 1863 the president of America will sign an Emancipation Proclamation freeing all the slaves in the confederacy. President Lincoln will be assassinated on Good Friday, 1865."

I suspect our first inclination would be to question the authenticity of the document, perhaps calling into question its alleged date. We would do so based upon the conviction that making such a specific prediction accurately is impossible. And we would be absolutely correct in concluding thus—it is humanly impossible to forecast the future with specificity. No one can do that. But what if after careful examination and analysis, the date was confirmed and the authenticity of the text was verified? That would be puzzling indeed. We find precisely this sort of predictive element in the Bible.[27] It is so startling that secularists and theological

25. Through Ramsey's work and testimony, typical critical views of the New Testament have been largely defeated. He wrote, "I began with a mind unfavorable to it (Acts), for the ingenuity and apparent completeness of the Tubingen theory had at one time quite convinced me. It did not lie then in my line of life to investigate the subject minutely; but more recently I found myself often brought into contact with the book of Acts as an authority for the topography, antiquities, and society of Asia Minor. It was gradually borne in upon me that in various details the narrative showed marvelous truth." Ramsay, *St. Paul the Traveller and Roman Citizen*, quoted in Geisler, *Christian Apologetics*, 326.

26. Scot McKnight, "Re-tracing Acts: Sir William Ramsey," 304–7.

27. "The great importance of the prophetic movement is evidenced by the occurrence of the word 'prophet' over 300 times in the OT and over 100 times in the NT. . . . Examination of the activities and writings of the prophets clarifies the OT prophetic

liberals have done their utmost to either laugh it away or explain it away. Critical scholars often attempt to condemn biblical prophecy by challenging the date, arguing that the predictive information was actually written by a reactor (an editor) after the fact to try and instill an appearance of the supernatural in Scripture. Thus they argue that alleged prophecy is actually nothing more than deceptive history.

For instance, the book of Isaiah appears to offer astounding predictions particularly in chapters 40–66. It is for this reason that many liberal scholars argue that Isaiah was actually the product of two or perhaps even three redactors. Many scholars believe that the predictive element of Isaiah mandates the existence of Deutero-Isaiah—a second, later author. The introduction to the book of Isaiah instructs the reader that the seer conducted his ministry during the tenure of four kings in Judah: Uzziah,

---

task. The OT prophet acted as a mouthpiece for God, receiving a message from Him and proclaiming it in accordance with His commands.... The position of a prophet differed from that of a king or a priest, who generally received their positions through heredity. No one could ever be a prophet simply because his father was one. Kings, priests, and other officials might be appointed or elected by human instrumentality.... No human individual or organization could enable a man to become a true prophet.... The prophet was not simply a wise man who gave good advice. He received a message from God and proclaimed it. Yet he was never a mere automaton through whom God caused words to be uttered. He was a human being facing real situations.... God revealed himself to the prophets in many ways. He used their personal observations and experiences as a means of preparing them to understand His messages. It is, however, the clear and definite teaching of the OT that the prophets received their message from God, so that it was His message, not theirs. Often the words were given them by direct revelation. In all cases the words in those messages that God desired to be preserved for future ages were inspired of the Holy Spirit to keep them from every type of error.... Until about 400 B.C., the prophetic movement was prominent in Israel. Time and again an individual came forward declaring the word of God, boldly facing political leaders and denouncing them for their sins, giving encouragement to God's people, or announcing God's will as to the next steps to be taken. After about 400 B.C. no more prophets appeared. There was no declaration that prophecy was ending, nor did anyone realize that this had occurred. Only after a time did realization dawn upon the people. The book of 1 Maccabees, which is on the whole a sober history of events during the Jewish revolt against Antiochus Epiphanes, brings out clearly in three places the fact that it was felt that there then was no prophet in Israel and that this had been true for a considerable length of time (1 Macc 9:27).... It is easy to see why God caused the OT prophetic movement to come to an end: (1) The entire OT had been written and its books were available as a guide for God's people. (2) It was God's will that an interval of about 400 years should elapse between the prophecies of the Messiah and his actual coming. *Although critics may assert that Daniel's prophecies were not written until after the events he so clearly predicted, no one can say that the many OT prophecies of Christ were written after the time when they were fulfilled*" [italics mine]. Tenney and Barabas, *Zondervan Pictorial Encyclopedia*, 4:875, 876, 878, 884, and 885.

Jotham, Ahaz, and Hezekiah. This means that he prophesied from about 740–680 B.C.

This period is well before the Babylonian exile that occurred in three stages from 605–586 B.C. and lasted until around 538 B.C. Now the quandary for liberal scholars will become apparent. In Isaiah 44:28—45:1 a very specific prediction is made. The text reads: "Who (the LORD) says of Cyrus, 'He is my shepherd and will accomplish all I please; he will say of Jerusalem, "Let it be rebuilt," and of the Temple, "Let its foundations be laid." ' This is what the LORD says to his anointed, to Cyrus, whose right hand I take hold of to subdue nations before him. . . ."

At the time of Isaiah's writing, Jerusalem had not been invaded by Babylon. That would not occur for another 100 years. Even more startling is the fact that Cyrus was the name of the king of the Medo-Persian Empire which would eventually defeat Babylon—but not until the 70-year captivity had concluded. Thus if Isaiah actually wrote this book sometime between 740–680 B.C. as is claimed in the introduction, he accurately predicted the name of the emancipator who would not even be born for over 100 years. Nor would he fulfill his mission for another 150 years! That is humanly impossible.

So, liberal scholars argue that the book of Isaiah could not have been the product of the genuine prophet, writing in the eighth century—at least not the last section.[28] But the evidence indicates otherwise.[29] The much

28. "When the higher criticism was applied to the OT, and scholars began to divide the Pentateuch into various alleged sources supposedly written at different times, a new dimension was added to the naturalistic efforts to explain the origin of the prophetical books. In 1789, Doederlein declared that Isaiah 40–66, which predicts the coming of Cyrus and the return of the Jews from exile, had been written more than a century after the time of Isaiah. Some of the same arguments that alleged that Isaiah could not have written chs. 40–66 were extended to various passages in the previous thirty-nine chapters. Eventually many critics divided the entire Book of Isaiah into great numbers of separate sections, allegedly written by a great variety of authors who were said to have lived at various times." Tenney and Barabas, *Zondervan Pictorial Encyclopedia*, 4:889. This was done principally out of convenience and an unwillingness to believe that prophets could actually forecast future events. But the internal testimony of Isaiah is quite cohesive and resistant to such attempts.

29. The Jewish historian, Josephus, writing in A.D. 93 affirmed the eighth-century date for Isaiah and endorsed his prediction of Cyrus as entirely legitimate writing. "In the first year of the reign of Cyrus . . . God commiserated the captivity and calamity of these poor people, according as he had foretold to them by Jeremiah the prophet, before the destruction of the city, that after they has [sic] served Nebuchadnezzar and his posterity, and after they had undergone that servitude seventy years, he would restore them

acclaimed Dead Sea Scrolls discovered in caves at Qumran, an Essene community, date from the second century B.C. They yielded a number of ancient scrolls; among them was a scroll of Isaiah. Liberal scholars expected that this scroll would indicate the activity of an editor—a Deutero-Isaiah. However, their expectation was disappointed. The scroll of Isaiah was complete with no break at chapter 39, indicating that all the chapters were authentic.[30]

Furthermore, Jewish tradition has uniformly viewed the entire text as the product of the eighth-century Isaiah. Now the Jewish priesthood was very well developed and acutely on guard against frauds and counterfeits. The fact that they accepted Isaiah indicates that oral tradition had endorsed the book in its entirety from its inception. Moreover, the Septuagint translators working in the second century B.C. also accepted it as a unified whole and translated it accordingly.[31] And it is clear that Jesus

---

again to the land of their fathers, and they should build their temple, and enjoy their ancient prosperity; and these things God did afford them; for he stirred up the mind of Cyrus, and made him write this throughout Asia:–'Thus saith Cyrus the King:–Since God Almighty hath appointed me to be king of the habitable earth, I believe that he is that God which the nation of the Israelites worship: for indeed he foretold my name by the prophets; and that I should build him a house at Jerusalem, in the country of Judea.' This was known to Cyrus by his reading the book which Isaiah left behind him of his prophecies; for this prophet said that God had spoken thus to him in a secret vision:–'My will is, that Cyrus, whom I have appointed to be king over many and great nations, send back my people to their own land, and build my temple. This was foretold by Isaiah one hundred and forty years before the temple was demolished. Accordingly, when Cyrus read this, and admired the divine power, an earnest desire and ambition seized upon him to fulfill what was so written; so he called for the most eminent Jews that were in Babylon, and said to them, that he gave them leave to go back to their own country, and to rebuild their city Jerusalem, and the temple of God, for that he would be their assistant, and that he would write to the rulers and governors that were in the neighborhood of their country of Judea, that they should contribute to them gold and silver for the building of the temple, and, beside that, beasts for their sacrifices." Whiston, *Josephus*, 480.

30. Indeed, the scroll entitled *1QIsaiaha* is a complete scroll of the book of Isaiah. It is seamless and contains all 66 chapters in 54 columns. Rather than a disruption at the conclusion of chapter 39, column 32 contains Isaiah 38:8—40:2 followed by column 33 which contains Isaiah 40:2–28. The prophecy of Cyrus is found in column 38 and the great Messianic prophecy of Isaiah 53 is recorded in column 44, including Isaiah 52:13—54:4. Based upon this evidence, it is certain that Isaiah chapters 1–66 were considered the authentic work of the eighth-century prophet, Isaiah. Martinez and Tigchelaar, *Dead Sea Scrolls*, 1:3–4.

31. The Septuagint (LXX) was the Greek translation of the Hebrew Old Testament Scriptures carried out due to the fear that the Jews would be increasingly Hellenized, losing their ability to read Hebrew—thus the need to perpetuate the Scripture in Greek.

believed in the authorship of Isaiah. In Luke 4:17–19, the gospel historian tells us that Jesus entered a synagogue, received the scroll of Isaiah, took it, and opened it to chapter 61. He then read verses 1–2, announcing that this prophecy had now been fulfilled.[32]

The internal evidence of the text further indicates that it is the product of a single author. Many of the same themes occur throughout the entire book. For instance, the title for God as "The Holy One of Israel" appears twelve times in chapters 1–39 and fourteen times in chapters 40–66. However, this title only occurs six other times in the entire Old Testament, indicating the work of the same author.[33] It is likely that the quibbling will continue over the appearance of the name of Cyrus, though to the candid mind it seems clear that the entire book is an eighth-century composition.

Nonetheless, there are prophecies in the book of Isaiah that are impervious to challenge based on date. They are undeniably before the fact—by hundreds of years—and this is true whether one dates Isaiah early or late. One of the most profound examples of this is the description of the work of God's Servant found in Isaiah chapter 53.[34] Prophetic literature by its nature is mysterious. It's a bit like looking across a foggy

---

32. Gaebelein, *Expositor's Bible Commentary*, 6:10–11.

33. Martin, "Isaiah," 1030. Martin identifies a number of other technical similarities in the two sections of Isaiah. "The 'highway' motif occurs in several parts of the book (Isa 11:16; 19:23; 35:8; 40:3; and 62:10). The 'remnant' theme occurs in 10:20-22; 11:11, 16; 28:5; 37:4; 37:32; and also in 46:3). . . . And 'peace' is mentioned 11 times in chapters 1–39 and 15 times in chapters 40–66. 'Joy' occurs 13 times in chapters 1–39 and 19 times in chapters 40–66. . . . The theological unity of the book argues for a single author," Martin rightly contends.

34. "One of the first to try to explain the prophetic movement from a naturalistic basis was Celsus, a writer who attacked Christianity in the 2nd cent. A.D. Celsus denied that the prophets had truly predicted the future. He dealt particularly with the Book of Daniel, claiming that its rather detailed predictions of Alexander the Great and his successors were not actually written until after the events had occurred, so that the alleged predictions were really based upon a later knowledge of what actually happened. This attitude toward the prophetic predictions has continued to the present time and has been a prominent factor in the attempts of modern critics to date many of the books much later than the time they claim to have been written. *It was done doubtless to forestall this sort of interpretation in relation to the most important predictions of the OT—those relating to the life and death of Christ—that God caused that the OT should be completed some centuries before the time of Christ to make it obvious that the OT predictions of Christ were made long before his time*" [italics mine]. Tenney and Barabas, *Zondervan Pictorial Encyclopedia*, 4:887.

field, seeing figures clearly but not faces. Even so, much can be ascertained with a relatively high degree of certainty. Isaiah 53 concerns God's Servant who is left unnamed. Even though his identity is not explicitly disclosed, we do learn several things about him. First, we learn that God's Servant is destined to suffer unto death. Second, we discover the purpose for his affliction. Both observations require further examination.

We encounter, by way of introduction, his unfortunate circumstances as a sufferer: "Just as there were many who were appalled at him, his appearance was so disfigured beyond that of any man and his form beyond human likeness" (Isa 52:14). Whatever his ordeal, it was surely horrific. The text continues to explain his plight in Isaiah 53:5 stating, "But he was pierced for our transgressions, he was crushed for our iniquities; the punishment that brought us peace was upon him, and by his wounds we are healed."

The very first term used to describe his torment is highly instructive. In Hebrew the word refers to a very precise kind of injury. It is a piercing wound.[35] Thus we learn that the Servant who is destined to suffer will be pierced. Other descriptive terms are used to articulate his affliction—he was "crushed"—a word that wields the idea of being broken in pieces.[36] Further, he was wounded, oppressed, afflicted, punished, stricken, and poured out unto death. Surely the scene is one of violence, bloodshed, punishment, execution. But the text informs us not only of what happens to God's Servant but why it occurs. The details here are clear, repetitive, and unambiguous. It is not as a result of his own crimes that he suffers. No, quite the contrary.

A close inspection of the passage yields nine instances that explicitly state that this Servant will suffer *for our sins*. Listen, "He was pierced for our transgression, he was crushed for our iniquities," "the LORD has laid on him the iniquity of us all," "for the transgression of my people he was stricken," "the LORD makes his life a guilt offering," "my righteous servant will justify many, and he will bear their iniquities," "and he was numbered with the transgressors. For he bore the sin of many, and made intercession for the transgressors" (Isa 53:5, 6, 8, 10, 11, and 12). I suggest that to the unbiased, the language of the text renders a startling predictive description

---

35. Brown, Driver, and Briggs. *Hebrew and English Lexicon*, 319. The word means "bore, pierce, . . . pierce through . . . hollow out . . . Isa 53:5 pierced, wounded for our transgressions."

36. Ibid., 193–4.

of the sacrifice of Messiah who would be punished as the perfect offering for sins—right down even to the piercing of the crucifixion.

This text offers a precise, definite, detailed forecast of the substitutionary work of God's Servant, one that could not have appeared after the fact. Isaiah was already a permanent fixture in the canonical literature well before the second century B.C. If this passage describes the work of Messiah, as seems likely, and if Messiah is identified as Jesus, Isaiah wrote this predictive report at least 200 years before Christ's passion. And no amount of tampering with dates can alter that fact.

When this prophecy is cross-referenced with one made by the prophet Daniel, the identity of this sufferer seems increasingly certain. Daniel was an exilic prophet. In other words, he conducted his ministry during the Babylonian exile in Babylon itself. In the first deportation conducted by the Babylonians in 605 B.C., they targeted youths who exhibited great promise, and Daniel was among them. Though unsupervised, Daniel remained faithful to the Lord, and God honored his fidelity with great success.

In chapter 9 of Daniel, we find the prophet studying the Scripture and specifically reading the prophet Jeremiah. He learned from this that the Babylonian captivity in which he lived was destined to extend only 70 years. Indeed, Jeremiah wrote in chapter 25:11–12 of his book: "This whole country will become a desolate wasteland, and these nations will serve the king of Babylon 70 years. But when the 70 years are fulfilled, I will punish the king of Babylon and his nation. . . ." And in Jeremiah 29:10 this promise is restated, "This is what the LORD says: 'When seventy years are completed for Babylon, I will come to you and fulfill my gracious promise to bring you back to this place.'"

Thus Daniel recognized that the captivity was drawing to a close.[37] He hoped to learn from God the future destiny of his people, Israel, following their release. So he went to prayer and asked God for help. He received substantially more than he likely expected. The text records, "While I was speaking and praying, and confessing my sin and the sin of my people Israel and making my request to the LORD my God . . .while I was still in prayer, Gabriel, the man I had seen in the earlier vision, came to me in

37. "Daniel took the seventy years literally and believed that there would be literal fulfillment. Even though Daniel was fully acquainted with the symbolic form of revelation which God sometimes used to portray panoramic prophetic events, his interpretation of Jeremiah was literal and he expected God to fulfill his word." Walvoord, *Daniel*, 205.

swift flight.... He instructed me and said to me, 'Daniel I have now come to give you insight and understanding'" (Dan 9:20–22).

The angelic messenger then provided Daniel with a concise synopsis of Israel's prophetic future. He announced, "Seventy 'sevens' (or weeks) are decreed for your people and your holy city.... Know and understand this: From the issuing of the decree to restore and rebuild Jerusalem until the Anointed One, the ruler, comes, there will be seven 'sevens,' and sixty-two 'sevens.' It will be rebuilt with streets and a trench, but in times of trouble. After the sixty-two 'sevens,' the Anointed One will be cut off and will have nothing" (Dan 9:24–26). It literally reads that seventy units of sevens are decreed. But what are these units of seven? They could refer to units of days or units of years or some other collective form of seven. However, there are good reasons to conclude that the term references units or bundles of seven years.[38]

First, we observe that Daniel was already thinking in terms of years as he was reading Jeremiah about the duration of the captivity. That was 70 years. So without any additional modifier, the most natural way for Daniel to interpret the units would be according to years. Furthermore, when the term referred to days in Daniel, it expressly stated it as such, as in Daniel 10:2, where it identifies the three units of seven as pertaining to days—or three weeks. Moreover, since it is the prophetic history of the Jewish people which was foretold, Daniel would have expected it to be a considerable period of time rather than delineated in days, weeks, or months. So a unit of seven years each is preferable.

Furthermore, God had commanded the people to allow the land to lie fallow every seventh year (Lev 25:1–7). However, they collectively failed to observe this condition. Thus they incurred God's wrath and he enforced the Sabbath rest on the land by removing the population. This

---

38. "The English word 'weeks' is misleading as the Hebrew is actually the plural of the word for *seven,* without specifying whether it is days, months, or years. The only system of interpretation, however, that gives any literal meaning to this prophecy is to regard the time units as prophetic years of 360 days each according to the Jewish custom.... The seventy times seven is, therefore, 490 years with the beginning at the time of 'the commandment to restore and to build Jerusalem' found in verse 25 and the culmination 490 years later." Ibid., 219–20. Members of the ancient church concurred in taking the seventy weeks or sevens as seventy units of seven years each. Origen wrote in his De Principiis, "The weeks of years, also, which the prophet Daniel had predicted extending to the leadership of Christ, have been fulfilled." Roberts and Donaldson, *Ante-Nicene Fathers,* 4:353.

was in fulfillment of the warning he issued in Leviticus 26:35 which states, "All the time that it (the land) lies desolate, the land will have the rest it did not have during the Sabbaths you lived in it." The Babylonian captivity lasted for 70 years because the people had forsaken the sabbatical land rest for 490 years (see 2 Chr 36:20-21). So, if the seventy units of seven refer to years, it is exactly parallel to the pre-captivity history of Judah in the Promised Land. I suspect that the seventy units of sevens refer to units of seven years each or to 490 years.

We further observe that this future period of time is subdivided into three sections: seven units of seven years, sixty-two units of seven years, and one unit of seven years.[39] It is helpful to remember that the prophecy referred to Daniel's people and the holy temple, so its focus is exclusively on the Jews. The seven sevens and the sixty-two sevens merge together and are viewed collectively (Dan 9:25). The first grouping of seven units of seven years equals 49 years and refers to the time necessary for the reconstruction and renovation process in Jerusalem following the captivity. Second Chronicles 36:19 describes the deplorable condition of the city following the razing of the Babylonians: "They set fire to God's temple and broke down the wall of Jerusalem; they burned all the palaces and destroyed everything of value there." It is not unreasonable to suppose that restoring order out of such mayhem would require several decades.

The sixty-two units of seven years each represent the span between the restoration of Jerusalem and the work of the Messiah (Dan 9:26). Thus we have an initial condition established of sixty-nine units of seven years each before the Messiah is "cut off." Sixty-nine sets of seven years equals 483 years. But in order for this eschatological clock to function meaningfully, we need a starting point. The angel Gabriel answered Daniel's question saying, "Know and understand this: From the issuing of the decree to restore and rebuild Jerusalem until the Anointed One (or Messiah), the ruler comes, there will be seven 'sevens' and sixty-two 'sevens' (or sixty-nine sevens or 483 years) . . . the Anointed One will be cut off and have nothing" [parentheses mine] (Dan 9:25).

But when was this decree to rebuild issued? There were several decrees made by Persian rulers in regard to the Jews and Jerusalem. The first appears in Ezra, chapter 1 and records the decree made by Cyrus in 538 B.C. But this order pertained very specifically to the rebuilding of the

---

39. For a fuller discussion of this accounting and prophecy see Pentecost, "Daniel," 1359–65 and Archer, "Daniel," 111–21.

temple (Ezra 1:1–5 and 2 Chr 36:22–23). So it is unlikely that this is the command in question.[40] But there was a decree issued by Artaxerxes in March of 444 B.C. that appears to fit the description (in the twentieth year of Artaxerxes in the month Nisan). Nehemiah had recently heard report of the dismal condition of the Jews in Jerusalem and had determined to assist (Neh 1).

In chapter 2, the king confronted Nehemiah about his downcast appearance and Nehemiah responded that he was upset that his homeland was still in ruins. Upon hearing this, the king inquired what Nehemiah wanted and was told, "If it pleases the king and if your servant has found favor in his sight, let him send me to the city in Judah where my fathers are buried that I may rebuild it" (Neh 2:5). Artaxerxes agreed to do so, making provisions for the appropriate lumber and other building supplies necessary for such a venture.

This is the decree that seems to correspond most precisely to the qualifications set forth by Gabriel. Fortunately, this date is established by both secular and sacred sources. King Artaxerxes reigned from 464–424 B.C., so the twentieth year of his reign was 444 B.C.[41] Furthermore, the month in which the decree was issued is also specifically stated as the month Nisan, which corresponds to March.

It appears that here the prophetic clock began ticking. The terminus point is identified as the time when the Anointed One is "cut off."

---

40. Archer rightly points out, "As we turn our attention to the *terminus a quo*, we note that v. 25 specifies the rebuilding of the city of Jerusalem with streets and moats, which will be completed within the forty-nine years. . . . The first possible fulfillment might be the first decree of Cyrus the Great (2 Chron 36:23; Ezra 1:2–4). Both versions of this decree stress just one undertaking: the rebuilding of the temple of Yahweh—a project in which Cyrus promised to cooperate with the Jewish leaders. . . . This says nothing about the restoring and building of the city as such. . . . It is most unlikely, then, that this decree can fulfill the specifications of v. 25." Archer, "Daniel," 113–4.

41. Regnal dates are somewhat imprecise, particularly when coregents ruled, as in the case of Nabonidus and Belshazzar. The king in Nehemiah is Artaxerxes I Longimanus the son and eventual successor of Xerxes or Ahasuerus as he is called in the book of Esther. Some biblical scholars commence the reign of Artaxerxes at 465 B.C. while others set it at 464 B.C. Thus a one-year discrepancy appears in their subsequent interpretations of this passage. One group of interpreters sets the date of the crucifixion at March A.D. 32 and the other at March A.D. 33. Either way, this prophetic forecast is startling in its degree of accuracy. The problem surrounding the exact date rests not with the prophet but with the interpreters. If all the facts were known precisely, the prophecy would no doubt correspond to the very day.

That term often refers to someone being killed by execution.[42] Note that Messiah will be cut off after the sixty-ninth week of years not during the seventieth week, indicating that there is an interval of time between the sixty-ninth and seventieth week (Dan 9:27). The Jewish calendar operated by a 360-day year. This is the reckoning typically employed when encountering eschatological predictions regarding Israel in Scripture.[43]

If one multiplies 483 years by 360 days, the final tally equals 173,880 days. This leads the interpreter to a date of March A.D. 33. Of course, it is very difficult to calculate the precise moment of the crucifixion of Jesus, but there is little doubt that this date is an amazingly close approximation.[44] This profound text indicates that Messiah, the Anointed One, the Christ, will be executed or cut off in or around the month of March A.D. 33.[45] Admittedly, this is a complicated text, one deserving close scrutiny. I

42. See Brown et al, *Hebrew and English Lexicon*, 504. *That person shall be cut off* (by death penalty).

43. Note especially the timeline set forth in the book of Revelation concerning the final unit of sevens or the future seven-year tribulation period, which states that forty-two months are the equivalent to 1260 days (see Revelation 11:2,3; 12:6; and 13:5). Sir Robert Anderson agrees regarding the last week or unit of sevens, "Now this seventieth week is admittedly a period of seven years, and half of this period is three times described as 'a time, times, and half a time,' or 'the dividing of time;' twice as forty-two months; and twice as 1,260 days. But 1,260 days are exactly equal to forty-two months of thirty days, or three and a half years of 360 days. . . . It is noteworthy that the prophecy was given at Babylon, and the Babylonian year consisted of twelve months of thirty days." Anderson, *Coming Prince*, 74–75.

44. Anderson has calculated the time in great detail explaining, "In accordance with the Jewish custom, the LORD went up to Jerusalem upon the 8th Nisan, 'six days before the Passover.' But as the 14th, on which the Paschal Supper was eaten, fell that year upon a Thursday, the 8th was the preceding Friday. He must have spent the Sabbath, therefore, at Bethany; and on the evening of the 9th, after the Sabbath had ended, the Supper took place at Martha's house. Upon the following day, the 10th Nisan, He entered Jerusalem as recorded in the Gospels. The Julian date of that 10th Nisan was Sunday the 6th April, A.D. 32. What then was the length of the period intervening between the issuing of the decree to rebuild Jerusalem and the public advent of 'Messiah the Prince,'—between the 14th March B.C. 445, and the 6th April A.D. 32? The interval contained exactly and to the very day 173880 days, or seven times sixty-nine prophetic years of 360 days, the first sixty-nine weeks of Gabriel's prophecy." Ibid., 127–8. While biblical scholars may differ slightly on the exact details, there is little variance among conservative scholarship as to the incisive character of this prophetic forecast.

45. Walvoord notes, "By far the majority of scholars who accept Daniel as a genuine book find the reference in verse 25 to Jesus Christ. . . . As this relates to the chronology of the prophecy, it makes plain that the Messiah will be living at the end of the sixty-ninth seven and will be cut off, or die soon after the end of it." Walvoord, *Daniel*, 229.

believe that the interpretation proposed treats the text with integrity and takes its message seriously.[46]

When the predictive message of Isaiah is combined with that of Daniel, a cohesive portrait emerges identifying Jesus as the object of prophetic fulfillment. Isaiah forecast his sufferings right down to the piercing wounds of the cross. Moreover, anyone who has a fundamental grasp on New Testament literature recognizes that the purpose for which the Servant suffered in Isaiah harmonizes precisely with it. Isaiah stated repeatedly that it was for our sins that the Servant would be punished. In this, the prophet Isaiah could easily be mistaken for the apostle Paul. Not only so, but Daniel provides the date when this sacrifice will occur.[47] In real history, the details of these two profound prophecies can only intersect at one person.

These are hardly the only prophecies in the Old Testament, but I think they suffice.[48] Since it is humanly impossible to accurately predict the future with any degree of specificity, the fact that Scripture consistently does so indicates that it is a unique product. Key representatives in the ancient and Reformation church believed that Scripture was divinely inspired; they believed this principally because of Scripture's commentary to that effect. Furthermore, its integrity in matters that can be tested is impressive. Its historical accuracy, geographic precision, and startling predictive ability all testify that the Scripture is a special composition whose message about the Designer should be carefully considered.

---

46. My treatment of this passage corresponds, if not in every detail, certainly in the major premise, with most of conservative biblical scholarship. For a particularly helpful commentary on Daniel see Walvoord, *Daniel: The Key to Prophetic Revelation*.

47. Anderson contends, "To believe that the facts and figures here detailed (regarding Daniel's prophecy of the 70 weeks) amount to nothing more than happy coincidences involves a greater faith than that of the Christian who accepts the book of Daniel as Divine" [parentheses mine]. Anderson, *Coming Prince*, 129.

48. Indeed, there are scores and scores of prophetic statements in Scripture, many of which have been fulfilled. One such prediction concerns the future return of the Christ penned by the prophet Zechariah. In Zechariah 12:10 the prophet reports on the Second Advent of Christ writing, ". . . They will look on me, the one they have pierced, and they will mourn . . ." The sacrificial work of the Messiah is prominent in this yet unfulfilled eschatological reference. Thus Zechariah and Isaiah concur that the Christ will be pierced in his sufferings. Zechariah wrote his prophecy over 400 years before Jesus was born.

3

Jesus the Christ: The Promised Messiah

O
F COURSE, JESUS CANNOT be the prophetic fulfillment of anything if he is merely a mythical character. I find it surprising that some people still think of him in those terms, most particularly since we have so much historical verification of his existence. Only the misinformed or the uninformed can possibly contend that Jesus is but a legend. As a matter of fact, if we know anything about the distant past, we know that a man named Jesus lived in the Near East during the first century who claimed to be the Christ, that he gathered a group of disciples together, and that he really was crucified by Pontius Pilate just as the biblical record attests.

But how do we know anything about the distant past? Our knowledge is generally based upon records; documents, histories, diaries, census reports, letters, or sometimes via archeological discoveries as in pottery, weapons, walls, bricks, etc. The past is revealed to us by means of records—written or otherwise. In the case of Jesus, we are fortunate to have abundant documentation from both sympathetic and unsympathetic witnesses. It has been said that the winners write history so it isn't always considered the unvarnished truth. However, historians typically agree that documentary evidence is particularly compelling if one finds the winners and the losers harmonizing regarding the facts under consideration. This is precisely the sort of unity one discovers when investigating the person of Jesus.

THE HISTORICITY OF THE CRUCIFIXION

Some might suspect that the sole evidence for the existence of Jesus is found in the Bible. That is incorrect. We do have thousands of ancient manuscripts, copies of the Gospels, documents of the New Testament, which were transcribed across time and space throughout the ancient world. These witnesses are typically viewed as sympathetic, the product of scribes who had a vested interest in their faith and sought to transmit the message of Christianity with integrity by copying the ancient records and distributing them and thus preserving the message.

Even though these records are from sympathetic transcribers, there is nothing devious about them. Indeed, textual criticism reveals that these copies are amazingly similar, such that it is abundantly apparent that they find their source in common originals.[1] These copies come from the early second century forward and are found all across the region of the ancient world.[2] In my Nestle-Aland Greek New Testament, there is a critical apparatus that identifies nearly every textual variant found between and among the manuscripts.[3]

1. ". . . some obtained from Egypt, some from Asia, and some from the West. The distances of the places and the numbers of the books show that they could not have been fabricated by collusion." Finegan, *Encountering New Testament Manuscripts*, 60.

2. Some preserved fragments are very small such as the oldest known papyrus fragment of any part of the New Testament, which dates around A.D. 125. It measures only about four inches by two inches in size. "On each side of the fragment are only seven lines of writing, and in each line only a few words or parts of words are preserved. Yet the characters are carefully written, and there is enough that is legible that a portion of the Gospel according to John can be recognized. As far as the words are preserved, they fall in the eighteenth chapter of the Gospel, in verses 31–33 and 37–38. Other, later manuscripts contain more of the text, or all of it. From them it is possible to reconstruct a complete text around the preserved portions on this fragment. Since the preserved words fit perfectly, a positive identification of the fragment is established." Ibid., 5.

3. We are not the least surprised to discover on a collation of manuscripts some minor variation between them. The work of a scribe was arduous indeed, and errors of the eye, ear, and hand occurred. However, the solidarity among the witnesses is impressive. None of the variants would alter any doctrine of the faith in the slightest degree. A brief excerpt from the critical apparatus provides a sense of the technical nature of the work and its helpful benefits to biblical scholars: "The apparatus always presents the witnesses in the same sequence: Greek, Latin, Syriac, Coptic, other witnesses, Church Fathers (separated from the preceding by a semicolon ;). The Greek witnesses also always follow a set sequence: papyri, uncials, minuscules, lectionaries. The uncials represented by letters of the alphabet Alpha, A, B, etc. come first in alphabetical order, followed by the rest in numerical order . . . with information on the majority text standing last." Nestle et al, *Novum Testamentum Graece*, 63. For a very helpful introduction to textual criticism, see Finegan, *Encountering New Testament Manuscripts*. Finegan observes regarding the presence of variants, "Nevertheless, in spite of the very real possibilities for corruption of the text in the course of its transmission, and the actual existence of many differences among the various manuscripts of the NT, the work of the copyists of the NT was, on the whole, done with great care and fidelity. It has, in fact, been seriously estimated that there are substantial variations in hardly more than a thousandth part of the entire text." Finegan, *Manuscripts*, 55.

If we possessed only the preserved Greek manuscripts of the New Testament, we would have an overabundance of documentary support about the historical legitimacy of Jesus. We would know beyond all reasonable doubt that he claimed to be the Christ, recruited disciples, suffered under Pilate, and was believed to have risen from the dead.[4] Indeed, one might reasonably argue that the crucifixion of Jesus is the best attested historical fact from antiquity.

However, we have important additional testimony in support of the evidence supplied by the New Testament documents. It would be historically irresponsible to relegate Jesus to mythology in light of the super-abundance of manuscript evidence to the contrary. Two prominent ancient historians, one Jewish and the other Roman, have left crucial records about the historicity of Jesus. This evidence is particularly significant because it comes from unfriendly witnesses. They had no interest in the Christian faith or its propagation. Their concern was historical not theological. Two particular passages from the work of Josephus, the Jewish historian, are of particular note. Josephus wrote his *Antiquities* around A.D. 93. In this work he sought to record the history of the Jewish people from the very beginning until his day.

One excerpt corroborates the historicity of Jesus and his half brother James. Josephus records:

> Festus was now dead, and Albinus was but upon the road; so he assembled the sanhedrin of judges, and brought before them the brother of Jesus, who was called Christ, whose name was James, and some others . . . and when he had formed an accusation against them as breakers of the law, he delivered them to be stoned.[5]

Several facts emerge. First, Jesus was a real person who was identified by some as Christ (or Messiah). Second, he had a brother named James; this is the same James who wrote the New Testament epistle of James.

---

4. These manuscripts are preserved in academic institutions, libraries, and museums throughout the world. The eminent New Testament scholar Bruce Metzger has calculated that between the uncial and minuscule manuscripts and lectionaries, the total number of existing Greek manuscripts, in part or in entirety, of the New Testament is 5,664. Metzger, "Documentary Evidence," 62–63. This immense documentary support far eclipses the manuscript evidence for any other work of antiquity. After the New Testament, the next best attested work is the *Iliad,* which is endorsed by some 650 Greek manuscripts, some of which are quite fragmentary.

5. Whiston, *Josephus*, 538.

Interestingly, he had apparently accepted martyrdom for his faith rather than recant. According to the biblical record, James did not become a believer in Jesus until following the crucifixion. What changed his opinion? According to 1 Corinthians 15:7 it was the resurrection that persuaded him to believe.

There is another text from Josephus that is even more startling. In it the Jewish historian confirms all the core claims presented by the gospel historians regarding Jesus:

> Now there was about this time Jesus, a wise man, if it be lawful to call him a man, for he was a doer of wonderful works—a teacher of such men as receive truth with pleasure. He drew over to him both many of the Jews, and many of the Gentiles. He was [the] Christ; and when Pilate at the suggestion of the principal men among us, had commended him to the cross, those that loved him at the first did not forsake him, for he appeared to them alive again the third day, as the divine prophets had foretold and ten thousand other wonderful things concerning him; and the tribe of Christians, so named from him, are not extinct at this day.[6]

Some scholars contend that sections of this entry are interpolations—they were added later by an editor.[7] While that is possible, the more salient point is that most scholars accept the bulk of this passage as authentic—that Josephus did write it. They acknowledge that Josephus considered Jesus a historically genuine figure. This offers striking corroborative evidence of the New Testament testimony about him. It reveals that Jesus made disciples of both Jews and Gentiles, that he was widely perceived as the Christ, that he was crucified by Pilate, and that the disciples demonstrated great fidelity as a result of his subsequent resurrection. That is impressive corroborative evidence.

And it is not only Josephus who validates the New Testament message. We find the same sort of endorsement from a Roman historian writing around A.D. 115 named Tacitus. He is considered one of the most

---

6. Ibid., 480.

7. For instance some contend that Josephus would not have accepted the miraculous work of Jesus or the reality of his resurrection. They argue that Josephus would have written that Jesus claimed to be Christ rather than that he was the Christ. But these are all somewhat tangential to the overall point; that most scholars accept the fact that Josephus actually wrote about Jesus affirming that he was crucified by Pilate and that the disciples claimed that he rose from the dead.

important historians of the ancient world and his comments are viewed as perhaps the most significant extra-biblical words about Jesus. He wrote:

> Nero fastened the guilt and inflicted the most exquisite tortures on a class hated for their abominations, called Christians by the populace. Christus, from whom the name had its origin, suffered the extreme penalty during the reign of Tiberius at the hands of one of our procurators, Pontius Pilate, and a most mischievous superstition, thus checked for the moment, again broke out not only in Judaea, the first source of the evil but even in Rome . . .[8]

These comments reinforce those made by the biblical writers precisely. Christ suffered the "extreme penalty," (which seems clearly an allusion to crucifixion), at the hands of Pilate just as the biblical record asserts. The "mischievous superstition" is likely a reference to the reported resurrection of Jesus.

These direct statements made by a disinterested witness are striking confirmation indeed. Hundreds of gospel records, thousands of New Testament documents, and direct support from two reliable unsympathetic historians—this is the sort of documentary support of which historians only dream. If anything from the distant past can be known with certitude, we know these core claims about Jesus to be true.

This coincides with the prophecies of both Isaiah and Daniel about the Servant, the Messiah, the Christ. Such a correlation is impressive. The Servant would be pierced, brutalized, and ultimately executed for our sins. This event would occur in March A.D. 33 according to Daniel, which harmonizes historically with the crucifixion of Jesus. Though all of this is verified beyond any reasonable doubt, the question remains: Was he really the Christ?

What could Jesus have done to prove that? Well, if he actually rose from the dead that would constitute pretty impressive evidence. But is there any possible way to evaluate that claim? In the history profession, when confronted with puzzling questions, we try to get to the primary sources for help. In this case, that leads us to the apostles of Christ, the primary witnesses of the resurrection.

8. Yamauchi, "Corroborating Evidence," 107–8.

THE LIKELIHOOD OF THE RESURRECTION

There is abundant evidence indicating that all of the apostles of Christ, save the traitor, invested their lives serving Jesus and endeavoring to build up the Christian Church following the crucifixion. Furthermore, the evidence suggests that many of the apostles suffered martyrdom for their faith. What is particularly impressive and significant about this fact is that the biblical record tells us that they were the very ones who claimed to have seen Jesus alive following the crucifixion. So they knew whether what they claimed was true or false.

Scripture portrays many of these confirmatory sightings as extending for long periods of time. Jesus ate meals together with the disciples following his passion and spent substantial time together instructing them. They are not depicted as brief encounters in which mistakes of identity could easily occur. On the second appearance in the upper room, Jesus invited doubting Thomas to examine his wounds carefully and verify his identity. Jesus did not appear to the apostles alone, but they are key primary sources—the firsthand witnesses. Now, people will sometimes surrender their lives for strongly held convictions. But would anyone suffer torture and martyrdom for something they knew categorically to be false? I contend that the activity of the apostles following the crucifixion is best explained by the resurrection.

Have you ever wondered why the authorities in charge at the time did not simply drag the body of Jesus through the streets to quell all this nonsense about the resurrection? He really was crucified—that is beyond doubt. Furthermore, the disciples really did claim that he appeared to them following his passion. That is a verifiable historical fact. If he did not rise from the dead, the authorities must have had his body. So why did the leaders fail to do what would have so obviously defeated all claims of resurrection? What could be simpler than that? I suggest that the most logical explanation for their lack of initiative in this regard is that they did not have his body. Thus they could not effectively check these rumors.

Some have argued that Jesus managed to survive the crucifixion and garner the strength to roll away the stone, escape the guards, and make his way to the disciples. But several factors make this idea far less than persuasive. First, the Romans were experts at torture and execution, and it is hardly conceivable that they failed to finish what they began. Second, one would not expect a brutalized individual to possess the fleetness of foot required to successfully flee from the guards. Keep in mind that the guards were charged with their lives to keep the tomb secure: If they lost the body, they would be put to death. Third, if Jesus had shown up in such a deplorable condition, it does not seem likely that he would have instilled the kind of courage and confidence indicative of the apostles subsequent to the event. This theory simply fails to convince.

Others have asserted that the disciples stole the body. We are asked to believe that they overpowered heavily armed professional soldiers, absconded with the body unseen, and successfully hid it somewhere beyond reach of the authorities. But if this is true, then the apostles knew their claims were false. And it becomes extremely difficult to explain their subsequent willingness to suffer for a cause they knew to be a lie. I do not think that this theory is compelling—particularly when we examine what history tells us happened to some of these apostles.

Clement of Rome lived in the first century. He was a contemporary of the apostles. He offers a brief account of the martyrdom of two chief apostles, Peter and Paul. While Clement explains the hazards of envy and how it resulted in their deaths, he wrote:

> Let us take the noble examples furnished in our own generation. Through envy and jealousy, the greatest and most righteous pillars have been persecuted and put to death. Let us set before our eyes the illustrious apostles. Peter, through unrighteous envy (not his own but his persecutors), endured not one or two, but numerous labors; and when he had at length suffered martyrdom departed to the place of glory due to him. Owing to envy, Paul also obtained the reward of patient endurance, after being seven times thrown into captivity, compelled to flee, and stoned. After preaching in both the east and west . . . suffered martyrdom under the prefects.[9]

Here we find two apostles who claimed to be firsthand witnesses of the resurrection choosing to suffer torture and eventual death rather than recant.

According to Clement, both Peter and Paul suffered for a long time before they were killed. Slow torture afforded them plenty of time to reconsider their position. Is it likely that these two men would have maintained their confession over long periods of time enduring extremely harsh treatment without capitulating, if it was for the sake of a lie—and

9. Roberts and Donaldson, *Ante-Nicene Fathers*, 1:6. One of the disputed epistles of St. Ignatius states that the martyrdom that Peter suffered was that of crucifixion. Ibid., 107.

one they knew full well was a lie? One might retort that perhaps they were just genuinely mistaken. This seems highly unlikely since they were the ones who testified of what they had seen—they were the primary sources. One might reason that they would have been very careful to assure themselves of the reliability of such encounters.

Peter's brother and fellow apostle, Andrew, was likewise tortured and martyred. As he stood before one named AEgeates, Andrew was asked to recant his faith in Jesus Christ, urged to support the pagan gods of the temple in Achaia, and offered release if he would do so. AEgeates stated:

> I compel thee to make a libation, that these people who have been deceived by thee may forsake the vanity of thy teaching, and may themselves offer grateful libations to the gods; for not even one city has remained in Achaia in which their temples have not been forsaken and deserted. And now, through thee, let them be again restored to the worship of the images, in order that the gods who have been enraged against thee, being pleased by this, may bring it about that thou may return to their friendship and ours. But if not, thou awaitest varied tortures, on account of the vengeance of the gods; and after these, fastened to the tree of the cross which thou commendest, thou shalt die.[10]

The same themes are prominent here; one finds an opportunity to abandon one's convictions regarding Christ and the reward is clemency. If not, threats followed, in this case the promise of torture and crucifixion. By the way, according to the record, a vast throng of witnesses accompanied Andrew throughout the ordeal—as many as twenty thousand people. That may seem exaggerated, but since the authorities wanted to intimidate and humiliate, it is not unreasonable to suppose they allowed spectators.

Andrew was hardly awed by these threats, responding with great courage and an uncompromising spirit:

> Listen, O son of death and chaff made ready for eternal burnings, to me, the servant of God and apostle of Jesus Christ. Until now I have conversed with thee kindly about the perfection of the faith, in order that thou, receiving the exposition of the truth . . . might despise vain idols and worship God, who is in the heavens; but since thou remainest in the same shameless at last, and thinkest me to be afraid because of thy threats, bring against me whatever

10. Roberts and Donaldson, *Ante-Nicene Fathers*, 8:513.

may seem greater in the way of tortures. For the more shall I be well pleasing to my king, the more I shall endure in tortures for the confession of his name.[11]

Following this lively confrontation, Andrew was strapped to a rack by twenty-one soldiers and stretched.[12] After being beaten, AEgeates offered another opportunity for freedom, which Andrew refused. At which point the exasperated and angry AEgeates ordered him to the cross. Some interpreters think Andrew was bound to the cross rather than nailed to it with spikes. The reason for their interpretation is found in the fact that he hung on this cross for three days. So that may well be the case, though it remains somewhat unclear in the text. In any event, Andrew preached for three days from the cross testifying of Jesus as the Christ.

Indeed, upon the fourth day the crowd grew agitated and began to demand his release. When it appeared that he would be brought down (which argues in favor of the bound not pierced interpretation), Andrew objected. He desired to see it through to the end—to give his life for Jesus Christ, believing that through his sacrifice others might also believe. He cried from the tree:

> Do not permit, O Lord, Thy servant at this time to be removed from Thee; for it is time that my body be committed to the earth, and Thou shalt order me to come to Thee. Thou who givest eternal life, my Teacher whom I have loved, whom on this cross I confess, whom I know, whom I possess, receive me, O Lord; as I have confessed Thee and obeyed Thee, so now in this word hearken to me; and before my body come down from the cross, receive me to Thyself, that through my departure there may be access to Thee of many of my kindred, finding rest for themselves in Thy majesty.[13]

His prayer was shortly thereafter answered and Andrew, like his brother, Peter, had suffered martyrdom.[14]

11. Ibid.

12. Following this episode, another opportunity to recant was offered, "Being stretched out, therefore, by seven times three soldiers, and beaten with violence, he was lifted up and brought before impious AEgeates. And he spoke to him thus: Listen to me, Andrew, and withdraw my thoughts from the outpouring of thy blood; but if thou wilt not hearken to me, I shall cause thee to perish on the tree of the cross." Ibid.

13. Ibid., 8:515.

14. As we have already seen, James, the half brother of Jesus, was stoned to death for his faith. Furthermore, James, the brother of John, was the slain victim of Herod the king according to Acts 12:1–2, and the fathers record that Bartholomew the apostle

While it is true that some of the details added by the fathers sound extreme, the executions themselves appear quite authentic. After all, this sort of opposition would be expected in the environment in which the apostles lived. They faced detractors on all sides, particularly from Roman polytheists and Jewish legalists. The emerging sect of Christianity represented an irritation to its Near Eastern neighbors, and it is not surprising that the attempt to silence them included targeting their leaders. The fact that none of these leaders deserted in the face of such hostilities is impressive. As we have seen, the opportunity to recant was a recurrent one.

Charles Colson considered such cohesive integrity compelling evidence to the authenticity of their claims. Colson was anticipating public embarrassment and possible prison time for his role in the Watergate scandal while he was considering the claims of Scripture concerning Jesus. When he contemplated the resolve of the apostles, he found it convincing. Colson knew that, when the Watergate scandal broke, all involved sought to escape punishment by making deals. No one stood firm. And in their case, they only feared relatively minor sanctions. But in the case of the apostles, they faced torture, humiliation, and execution. Yet none of them plea bargained, no one recanted, nobody deserted, everyone stood firm for their testimony—even unto death. Why did they do so? To my mind, the most satisfactory explanation for their actions is the resurrection. They really did see the risen Christ, just as they had claimed. Charles Colson reached the same verdict.[15]

---

also suffered martyrdom by being beaten and then beheaded. Moreover, the apostle John was banished to the isle of Patmos for his faith, and there he received the book of Revelation.

15. Colson explains his reasoning, "History reveals that after the criminal investigation of the White House began—as it did with Dean's April 8 meeting with the prosecutors—the end of Mr. Nixon's presidency was only a matter of time. The cover-up was discovered—and doomed—and this is why the dates are so important. For though the cover-up technically dated back to the June 1972 break-in, the serious cover-up—the part everyone knew or should have known was criminal—really began March 21, 1973. And it ended April 8, 1973. With the most powerful office in the world at stake, a small band of hand-picked loyalists, no more than ten of us, could not hold a conspiracy together for more than two weeks. . . . If John Dean and the rest of us were so panic-stricken, not by the prospects of beatings and execution, but by political disgrace and a possible prison term, one can only speculate about the emotions of the disciples. Unlike the men in the White House, the disciples were powerless people, abandoned by their leader, homeless in a conquered land. Yet they clung tenaciously to their enormously offensive story that their leader had risen from His ignoble death and was alive—and was *the* Lord. The Watergate cover-up reveals, I think, the true nature of humanity. None of the memoirs

The documentary evidence attesting to the life and death of Jesus is greater than that which exists for any other figure from the distant past. His crucifixion at the hands of Pilate is a historical fact. Indeed, if any event from the ancient world can be considered incontestable, it would be his execution at the cross. We also know that Jesus was considered the Christ by his followers. Furthermore, it is historically clear that his apostles expressed great fidelity to Jesus as the Promised One from God, even following his crucifixion.

They unanimously voiced the reason for their steadfast allegiance as being the resurrection. The apostles claimed that they saw Jesus following his passion, alive and well. They testified that Jesus ate with them, taught them, and directly commissioned them to take the gospel into the world. Thus they are key primary sources. They knew if what they claimed was true or false. Based upon their subsequent actions, it is reasonable to accept their testimony as reliable. As a matter of fact, no other theory satisfactorily explains their sacrifices.

THE COHERENT THEME OF THE BIBLE

When such historical certitude is combined with the assertions of Scripture, its testimony is multiplied considerably. We have seen that Isaiah predicted the manner in which Messiah would suffer—right down to the piercing of the crucifixion. The seer also articulated repeatedly why Christ would suffer—for our sins. The prophet Daniel predicted when all of this would occur—March A.D. 33. This harmonizes with the historical facts surround-

---

suggest that anyone went to the prosecutor's office out of such noble notions as putting the Constitution above the President, or bringing rascals to justice, or even moral indignation. Instead, the writings of those involved are consistent recitations of the frailty of man. Even political zealots at the pinnacle of power will save their own necks in the crunch, though, it may be at the expense of the one they profess to serve so zealously. Is it really likely, then, that a deliberate cover-up, a plot to perpetuate a lie about the Resurrection, could have survived the violent persecution of the apostles . . . ? Is it not probable that at least one of the apostles would have renounced Christ before being beheaded or stoned? . . . Surely one of the conspirators would have made a deal with the authorities (government and Sanhedrin probably would have welcomed such a soul with open arms and pocketbooks!). . . . Take it from one who was inside the Watergate web looking out, who saw firsthand how vulnerable a cover-up is: Nothing less than a witness as awesome as the resurrected Christ could have caused those men to maintain to their dying whispers that Jesus is alive and Lord. This weight of evidence tells me the apostles were indeed telling the truth: Jesus rose bodily from the grave. . . ." Colson, *Loving God*, 66–69.

ing the execution of Jesus with startling precision. It appears from these prophetical writings that the cross was a preordained appointment.[16]

These Messianic predictions, made hundreds of years before Jesus arrived, are at the very heart of the Bible. Indeed, the theme of Scripture is redemption through sacrifice and most especially the sacrifice of the Christ. The very first Passover, conducted while the Israelites were still in bondage to Egypt, is representative.

In Exodus, chapter 12, God explained how the Jewish people could escape the destroyer who would ravage Egypt. He commanded that a spotless lamb be slain and that the blood of the lamb should be sprinkled upon their doorposts. They were to remain inside on the evening of judgment. The text states: "The blood will be a sign for you on the houses where you are; and when I see the blood, I will pass over you. No destructive plague will touch you when I strike the land of Egypt" (Exod 12:13). Because of the shed blood, God's judgment passed over them.

The entire Jewish sacrificial system looked forward to a permanent remedy for the sin problem. With the completion of the Tabernacle and later the Temple, the High Priest had access to the Holy of Holies on but one day per year, on Yom Kippur or The Day of Atonement. After sacrificing for his own sins, the High Priest entered beyond the veil and sprinkled the blood of the sacrifice upon the Mercy Seat (the cover of the Ark of the Covenant), making atonement for the sins of the nation. Of course, this holy ceremony, like all the other sacrifices and festivals prescribed in the Old Testament, demanded repetition. The chasm between God and sinful human beings could never be finally defeated by these sacrifices. They provided a temporary, not an ultimate, reprieve. So the Jews awaited the final answer.

The purpose of the gospel historians was to present Jesus as the answer, the Christ, the final solution. The Gospels are not biographical. Indeed,

---

16. It isn't as though the crucifixion of Jesus occurred and the apostles sought to make the best of it. The prophets had foretold its occurrence and then it happened. Using a helpful analogy employed by Dembski, flipping a coin one hundred times would produce an unlikely arrangement of heads and tails—but it would be an order that came about entirely by chance. However, to accurately predict the order of heads and tails for one hundred successive coin flips in advance and then to achieve that order precisely is something else again. Complexity-specification criteria make such an event highly unlikely—and I contend that the same principle holds true for the predictions of when, how, and why Christ would suffer. It is this sort of forecast fulfillment that effectively removes chance as an explanatory mechanism for the crucifixion of Jesus.

other than the birth narratives, Luke only mentions the early life of Jesus once (Luke 2:40–52). The gospel of John devotes fully one third of the text to the last week in the life of Jesus and his subsequent resurrection (John 12–21). Furthermore, John stated the purpose for his letter directly, saying, "But these are written that you may believe that Jesus is the Christ, the Son of God, and that by believing you may have life in his name" (John 20:31).

What is true of John is true of all. Matthew sought to convince the Jews that their Messiah had come, and this explains the many allusions to fulfilled prophecy expressed in his gospel. Mark endeavored to convince the Romans of the uniqueness of Jesus. Thus he emphasized the activity of Christ, especially his miraculous work. Finally, Luke tried to reason with the Greeks about the special nature of Jesus as the Christ. All of the gospel historians had the same purpose in mind presenting Jesus as the Promised One from God who would solve the sin problem with finality.

The book of Acts is the historical recounting of the propagation of the gospel throughout the ancient world in the first century. This mission was incited by the risen Christ (Acts 1:8) who enjoined his followers to take the gospel to Jerusalem (Acts 1–7), Judea, and Samaria (Acts 8–14), and to the uttermost parts of the world (Acts 16–28). The message of the apostles, the primary witnesses, was constantly the same—Jesus was the promised Christ who suffered for sins, and rose again from the dead.

They affirmed the exclusivity of the gospel—faith in Christ alone— in many passages. Acts 4:12 is illustrative where Peter declared regarding Jesus, "Salvation is found in no one else, for there is no other name under heaven given to men by which we must be saved" (Acts 4:12). Paul stated precisely the same thing when the jailer at Philippi inquired how to be made right with God, "Believe in the Lord Jesus and you will be saved. . . ." (Acts 16:31).

Anyone who is familiar with the writings of the church letters is aware that the sacrifice of Christ at the cross for sins and his subsequent resurrection pervades the documents.[17] This theme is so thoroughly

---

17. Let me offer a concise summary: The gospel or "good news" from God consumed the teaching and preaching ministry of the apostle Paul. In Rom 1:16 he stated, "I am not ashamed of the gospel, because it is the power of God for the salvation of everyone who believes, . . ." And again to the Corinthians he explicitly noted that communicating the gospel message was his passion, "For Christ did not send me to baptize, but to preach the gospel—not with words of human wisdom, lest the cross be emptied of its power" (1 Cor 1:17). Furthermore, the apostle succinctly defined this gospel from God writing, "Now, brothers, I want to remind you of the gospel I preached to you. . . . For what I received I passed on to

you as of first importance: *that Christ died for our sins*, according to the Scriptures, that he was buried, and that he was raised on the third day according to the Scriptures, and that he appeared to Peter, and then to the twelve [italics mine]. After that, he appeared to more than five hundred of the brothers at the same time, most of whom are still living, though some have fallen asleep. Then he appeared to James (his half brother), then to all the apostles, and last of all he appeared to me . . . " [parentheses mine] (1 Cor 15:1, 3–7). The gospel pervaded Paul's thoughts as he iterated the theme of salvation by faith in the work of Jesus the Christ constantly in his letters. A brief sampling makes this abundantly clear: "But now a righteousness from God, apart from law, has been made known, to which the law and the Prophets testify. This righteousness from God comes through faith in Jesus Christ to all who believe. There is no difference (between Jews and Gentiles), for all have sinned and fall short of the glory of God, and are justified freely by his grace through the redemption that came by Jesus Christ" [parentheses mine] (Rom 3:21–24); "We are therefore Christ's ambassadors, as though God were making his appeal through us. We implore you on Christ's behalf: Be reconciled to God. God made him (Jesus) who had no sin to be sin for us, so that in him we might become the righteousness of God" [parentheses mine] (2 Cor 5:20–21); "The life I live in the body, I live by faith in the Son of God, who loved me and gave himself for me. I do not set aside the grace of God, for if righteousness could be gained through the law, Christ died for nothing" (Gal 2:20–21); "In him (Jesus) we have redemption through his blood, the forgiveness of sins" [parentheses mine] (Eph 1:7); "But whatever was to my profit I now consider loss for the sake of Christ. What is more, I consider everything a loss compared to the surpassing greatness of knowing Christ Jesus my Lord, for whose sake I have lost all things. I consider them rubbish, that I may gain Christ and be found in him, not having a righteousness of my own that comes from the law, but that which is through faith in Christ—the righteousness that comes from God by faith" (Phil 3:7–9); "When you were dead in your sins . . . God made you alive with Christ. He forgave us all our sins, having canceled the written code, with its regulations, that was against us and that stood opposed to us; he took it away, nailing it to the cross" (Col 2:13–14); "Here is a trustworthy saying that deserves full acceptance: Christ Jesus came into the world to save sinners—of whom I am the worst. But for that very reason I was shown mercy so that in me, the worst of sinners, Christ Jesus might display his unlimited patience as an example for those who would believe on him and receive eternal life" (1 Tim 1:15–16); "At one time we too were foolish, disobedient, deceived and enslaved by all kinds of passions and pleasures. We lived in malice and envy, being hated and hating one another. But when the kindness and love of God our Savior appeared, he saved us, not because of righteous things we had done, but because of his mercy. He saved us through the washing of rebirth and renewal by the Holy Spirit, whom he poured out on us generously through Jesus Christ our Savior" (Titus 3:3–7).

The grace and mercy of God through the gift of Jesus the Christ permeated Paul's thinking. This is the gospel. The theme is always the same: sinners are invited to trust in Jesus the Christ who died for our sins and rose again, making forgiveness possible. This is the heart of Paul's message. Of course, this message is in seamless harmony with the predictive forecasts of the prophets regarding Christ and the portrayal of Jesus as the Christ by the gospel writers. The predictions of Isaiah and Daniel were essentially etched in stone as part of the inspired corpus. They agreed that Messiah would be executed, with Isaiah adding details as to how and why and Daniel as to when. The gospel historians wrote in order to identify Jesus as the promised Christ. Jesus really was crucified under Pilate—a fact that is historically incontestable. The apostles claimed to have seen him

embedded in Pauline literature that to extract its essence from any book would leave little more than a brief salutation and a terse farewell. The most comprehensive letter is his book of Romans. In it, Paul argued for the universal need of the gospel. In the climax of the first movement of his argument Paul states:

> But now a righteousness from God, apart from the law, has been made known, to which the Law and the Prophets testify. This righteousness from God comes through faith in Jesus Christ to all who believe. There is no difference (between Jews and Gentiles), for all have sinned and fall short of the glory of God, and are justified freely by his grace through the redemption that came by Christ Jesus. God presented him as a sacrifice of atonement, through faith in his blood [parentheses mine] (Rom 3:21–25).

Further examples of this sentiment could be multiplied to a great extent throughout the Pauline corpus. It is a fair assessment to conclude that salvation by faith in Jesus Christ and his atoning sacrifice at the cross *is* the Pauline message. We can add nothing to the work of Christ—we can only trust in him as the perfect sacrifice, Paul constantly urged.

The apostle Peter had the same message to proclaim to his audience. Peter wrote, "For you know that it was not with perishable things such as silver and gold that you were redeemed from the empty way of life handed down to you from your forefathers, but with the precious blood of Christ, a lamb without blemish or defect" (1 Pet 1:18–19). The anonymous writer of the book of Hebrews eloquently argues for the superiority of Christ over angels, Moses, the Jewish priesthood, and the sacrificial system of Judaism. Christ is the answer—the final solution. When contrasting the superiority of Christ to the Jewish priesthood, he observed, "Day after day every priest stands and performs his religious duties; again and again he offers the same sacrifices, which can never take away sins. But when this

---

alive following his passion. As the primary witnesses they knew the truth substantiating their claims. The remainder of the New Testament is a unanimous and unremitting testimony of these central claims. This coherence defies chance. Taken collectively, the message is far too specified and complex to be anything other than the product of a brilliant design. Indeed, it would appear that the cross was a divine appointment. The theme of the Bible is redemption through sacrifice, and most particularly redemption through the sacrifice of the Christ, the Promised One from God—the Messiah—Jesus. Forecast by the seers, affirmed by the gospel witnesses, and confirmed constantly throughout the New Testament by the apostles—even unto death. To suppose that all of these historical details are the product of chance is quite literally beyond all reason.

priest (Jesus) had offered for all time one sacrifice for sins, he sat down at the right hand of God" [parentheses mine] (Heb 10:11–12).

The redundancy of the Old Covenant priesthood is starkly contrasted with the finality of the work of Christ. By one offering, the atoning work is completed, finished. Thus Christ is seated never to be offered again. His work is done. Hence the author argues it is far better than the perpetual rituals of Judaism. Lastly, we note that the apostle John harmonized with the rest. As we have seen, his gospel explicitly stated the purpose for his writing—to present Jesus as the Christ. In the Apocalypse he reaffirmed this message, "To him who loves us and has freed us from our sins by his blood, and has made us to be a kingdom and priests to serve his God and Father—to him be glory and power for ever and ever!" (Rev 1:5).

The residents of heaven praise Christ for his great atoning sacrifice. He alone is worthy, they declare, to open the seven-sealed book, which commences the Tribulation Period on earth. John gives them utterance as he records their words of adoration, "And they sang a new song: You are worthy to take the scroll and to open its seals, because you were slain and with your blood you purchased men for God from every tribe and language and people and nation" (Rev 5:9).

The Old Testament looked forward to the coming of the Christ, the gospels present Jesus as the Christ, and the rest of the New Testament categorically affirms this identity, proclaiming forgiveness of sins through faith in the sacrificial work of Jesus the Christ. This solidarity from an ancient composition produced over a period of some 1600 years and including literature from over 40 different writers is striking. All this indicates that Scripture is a unique composition whose message about the Designer should be carefully considered.

CONCLUSION

I have argued that theism is a far more compelling option than atheism—intellectually, logically, and rationally superior. Once God is admitted, one might reasonably expect some form of revelatory communication to exist. I contend that the Scripture is this communiqué, a unique composition demonstrating its special character in a number of profound ways, most particularly by its fidelity in matters which can be tested and its ability to successfully forecast future events with specificity. Since it is humanly impossible to accurately predict the future with any degree of precision, the fact that Scripture does so confirms its divine character.

While the Bible speaks about lots of things, the heart of its message is redemption through sacrifice, and especially the sacrifice of Christ. This is the coherent theme of Scripture, and Jesus is consistently identified as the Christ. This claim is affirmed by his life and his death, suffering at precisely the time and in exactly the manner prescribed by the prophets. The cohesive message of the apostles—the primary sources—following the crucifixion, even under considerable duress, further testifies to the reality of the bodily resurrection of Christ. To my mind, when these facts are viewed collectively, the Christian faith is endorsed by a considerable amount of compelling evidence, making its truth claims quite probable, intellectually satisfying, and entirely reasonable.

Bibliography

Alexander, Archibald. *Evidences of the Authenticity, Inspiration, and Canonical Authority of the Holy Scriptures.* Philadelphia: Presbyterian Board of Publications, 1837.

———. "Review of Woods on Inspiration." *Biblical Repertory And Theological Review* 3 (January 1831) 3–22.

Anderson, Sir Robert. *The Coming Prince.* Grand Rapids: Kregel, 1984.

Archer, Gleason. "Daniel." In *The Expositor's Bible Commentary,* edited by Frank E. Gaebelein. 12 vols. Grand Rapids: Zondervan, 1986.

Barrow, John D., and Frank J. Tipler. *The Anthropic Cosmological Principle.* New York: Oxford University Press, 1986.

Barrows, E.P. "The Alleged Disagreement between Paul and James." *Bibliotheca Sacra* 9 (1852) 761–82.

Behe, Michael J. *Darwin's Black Box: The Biochemical Challenge to Evolution.* New York: The Free Press, 1996.

———, William A. Dembski, and Stephen C. Meyer. *Science and Evidence for Design in the Universe.* San Francisco: Ignatius Press, 2000.

Bernasconi, Robert, and Tommy L. Lott. *The Idea of Race.* Cambridge: Hackett Publishing, 2000.

Brown, Francis, S.R. Driver, and Charles A. Briggs. *A Hebrew and English Lexicon Of the Old Testament.* Oxford: Clarendon Press, 1980.

Bryson, Bill. *A Short History of Nearly Everything.* New York: Broadway Books, 2003.

Cairns-Smith, A.G. *Seven Clues to the Origin of Life.* New York: Cambridge University Press, 1985.

Collins, Robin. "The Evidence of Physics: The Cosmos on a Razor's Edge." In *The Case for a Creator,* by Lee Strobel. Grand Rapids: Zondervan, 2004.

Colson, Charles W. *Loving God.* Grand Rapids: Zondervan, 1983.

"The Conflict between Religion and Science." *Andover Review* (1890) 450–55.

Corner, E. J. H. "Evolution." In *Contemporary Botanical Thought,* edited by Anna M. MacLeod and L.S. Cobley. Chicago: Quadrangle Books, 1961.

"The Cosmogony of Genesis: Professor Driver's Critique of Professor Dana." *Bibliotheca Sacra* 45 (1888) 356–65.

Craig, William Lane. *The Kalam Cosmological Argument.* London: The MacMillian Press, 1979.

———, and J. P. Moreland, eds. *Naturalism: A Critical Analysis.* New York: Routledge, 2000.

Cutting, Sewall S. "Geology and Religion." *Christian Review* 15 (1850) 380–99.

Dana, Jay J. "The Religion of Geology." *Bibliotheca Sacra* 10 (1853) 505–22.

Darwin, Charles. *The Origin of Species.* New York: Gramercy Books, 1979.

Davis, Percival, and Dean H. Kenyon. *Of Pandas and People: The Central Question Of Biological Origins.* Dallas: Haughton Publishing, 1993.

Dawkins, Richard. *The Blind Watchmaker.* Boston: Houghton Mifflin Co., 2008.

Dembski, William A. *The Design Inference: Eliminating Chance Through Small Probabilities.* New York: Cambridge University Press, 1998.

———. *No Free Lunch: Why Specified Complexity Cannot be Purchased Without Intelligence.* Lanham, MD: Rowan and Littlefield, 2002.

———. *Uncommon Dissent: Intellectuals Who Find Darwinism Unconvincing.* Wilmington, DE: ISI Books, 2004.

———. "Naturalism and Design." In *Naturalism: A Critical Analysis,* edited by William Lane Craig and J. P. Moreland. New York: Routledge, 2000.

———, and James M. Kushiner. *Signs of Intelligence: Understanding Intelligent Design.* Grand Rapids: Brazo Press, 2001.

———, and Jonathan Wells. *The Design of Life. Discovering Signs of Intelligence in Biological Systems.* Dallas: Foundation for Thought and Ethics, 2008.

Denton, Michael. *Evolution: A Theory in Crisis.* Bethesda, MD: Adler & Adler, 1986.

Dick, John. *An Essay on the Inspiration of the Holy Scriptures of the Old and New Testaments.* Boston: Lincoln and Edwards, 1811. (On microprint American Antiquarian Society at the University of Rochester).

Edwards, B.B. "Messianic Prophesies." *Bibliotheca Sacra* 9 (1852) 609–22.

Finegan, Jack. *Encountering New Testament Manuscripts.* Grand Rapids: Eerdmans, 1974.

Gaebelein, Frank E., ed. *The Expositor's Bible Commentary.* 12 vols. Grand Rapids: Zondervan, 1986.

Geisler, Norman. *Christian Apologetics.* Grand Rapids: Baker, 1976.

"Geographical Accuracy of the Bible." *Christian Review* 20 (1855) 451–61.

Gills, James P., and Tom Woodward. *Darwinism Under the Microscope: How Recent Scientific Evidence Points to Divine Design.* Lake Mary, FL: Charisma House, 2002.

Gingerich, Owen. "Dare a Scientist Believe in Design?" In *Evidence of Purpose,* edited by John Marks Templeton. New York: Continuum, 1994.

Gould, Stephen Jay. *Wonderful Life: The Burgess Shale and the Nature of History.* New York: W.W. Norton & Company, 1989.

———. *The Mismeasure of Man.* New York: W.W. Norton, 1996.

Harris, Errol E. *Cosmos and Theos: Ethical and Theological Implications of the Anthropic Cosmological Principle.* New Jersey: Humanities Press, 1992.

Hitchcock, Edward. "The Connection between Geology and the Mosaic History of Creation." *Biblical Repository* 5 (1835) 439–51.

Hodge, A. A., and B. B. Warfield. "Inspiration." *Presbyterian Review* 6 (1881) 226–60.

Hodge, Charles. Review of *The Inspiration of Holy Scripture: Its Nature and Proof,* by William Lee. *Princeton Review* 29 (October 1857) 660–98.

———. *Systematic Theology.* 3 vols. Reprint of 1871–1873 edition. Grand Rapids: Eerdmans, 1981.

———. *What is Darwinism?* New York: Scribner, Armstrong, and Company, 1874.

Jaki, Stanley. *Science and Creation.* New York: Science History Publications, 1974.

Johnson, F. H. "Reason and Revelation." *Andover Review* 5 (1886) 229–49.

Johnson, Phillip E. *Darwin on Trial.* Washington, DC: Regnery Gateway, 1991.

———. *The Wedge of Truth: Splitting the Foundations of Naturalism.* Downers Grove, IL: InterVarsity Press, 2000.

Ladd, George T. *The Doctrine of Sacred Scripture.* 2 vols. Edinburgh: T. and T. Clark, 1883.

Lee, William. *The Inspiration of Holy Scripture: Its Nature and Proof.* New York: Robert Carter and Brothers, 1857.

Lewontin, Richard. "Billions and Billions of Demons." *New York Review of Books* (January 9, 1997) 31.

Lord, David N., ed. "The Inspiration of the Scriptures: Its Nature and Extent." *Theological and Literary Journal* 10 (July 1857) 1–45.

MacLeod, Anna M., and L.S. Cobley, eds. *Contemporary Botanical Thought.* Chicago: Quadrangle Books, 1961.

Martin, John A. "Isaiah." In *The Bible Knowledge Commentary*, edited by John F. Walvoord and Roy B. Zuck. 2 vols. Grand Rapids: Victor, 1986.

Martinez, Florentino Garcia, and Eibert J.C. Tigchelaar. *The Dead Sea Scrolls.* 2 vols. Grand Rapids: Eerdmans, 1997.

McKnight, Scot. "Re-tracing Acts: Sir William Ramsey." In *More than Conquerors*, edited by John Woodbridge, 304–7. Chicago: Moody Press, 1992.

Metzger, Bruce. "The Documentary Evidence." In *The Case for Christ*, by Lee Strobel. Grand Rapids: Zondervan, 1998.

Meyer, Stephen C. "The Evidence of Biological Information: The Challenge of DNA and the Origin of Life." In *The Case for a Creator*, by Lee Strobel. Grand Rapids: Zondervan, 2004.

Mooreland, P.S., and M.M. Kaplan, eds. *Mathematical Challenges to the Neo-Darwinian Interpretation of Evolution.* Philadelphia: Wistar Institute Press, 1967.

Morris, Henry M., and Gary E. Parker. *What is Creation Science?* Green Forrest, AR: Master Books, 1996.

Mosse, George L. *Toward the Final Solution: A History of European Racism.* New York: Howard Fertig, 1985.

Nestle, Eberhard, Erwin Nestle, and Kurt Aland, eds. Novum Testamentum Graece. 26th ed. Stuttgart: Deutsche Bibelstiftung, 1979.

Pentecost, J. Dwight. "Daniel." In *The Bible Knowledge Commentary*, edited by John F. Walvoord and Roy B. Zuck. Wheaton: Victor Books, 1985.

Pond, Enoch. Review of *The Inspiration of Holy Scripture: Its Nature and Proof*, by William Lee. *Bibliotheca Sacra* 15 (1858) 29–54.

———. "Alleged Discrepancies in the Bible." *Christian Review* 23 (1858) 380–415.

"The Religion of Geology." *Bibliotheca Sacra* 17 (1860) 673–709.

Roberts, Alexander, and James Donaldson, eds. *Ante-Nicene Fathers: The Writings of the Fathers Down to A.D. 325.* 10 vols. Peabody, MA: Hendrickson Publishers, 1995.

Robertson, A.T. *A Grammar of the Greek New Testament in Light of Historical Research.* Nashville: Broadman, 1934.

Robinson. "Rawlinson's Historical Evidences." *Christian Review* 25 (July 1860) 499–518.

Ross, Hugh. *The Creator and the Cosmos: How the Greatest Scientific Discoveries of the Century Reveal God.* Colorado Springs: Nav Press, 1993.

———. *The Fingerprint of God: Recent Scientific Discoveries Reveal the Unmistakable Identity of the Creator.* Orange, CA: Promise Publishing Company, 1991.

Sanday, William. *Inspiration: Eight Lectures on the Early History and Origin of the Doctrine of Biblical Inspiration.* London: Longmans, Green, and Company, 1893.

Satta, Ronald F. *The Sacred Text: Biblical Authority in Nineteenth-Century America.* Eugene, OR: Pickwick Publications, 2007.

———. "The Case of Professor Charles A. Briggs: Inerrancy Affirmed." *Trinity Journal* 26 (2005) 69–90.

———. "Fundamentalism and Inerrancy: A Response to the Sandeen Challenge." *Evangelical Journal* 21 (2003) 66–80.

———. "Inerrancy: The Prevailing Orthodox Opinion of the Nineteenth-Century Theological Elite." *Faith and Mission Journal* 24 (2007) 79–96.

Schaff, Philip, and Henry Wace, eds. *Nicene and Post-Nicene Fathers*. 14 vols. Peabody, MA: Hendrickson Publishers, 1995.

Schutzenberger, Marcel. "Algorithms and Neo-Darwinian Theory of Evolution." In *Mathematical Challenges to the Neo-Darwinian Interpretation of Evolution*, edited by P. S. Mooreland and M.M. Kaplan. Philadelphia: Wistar Institute Press, 1961.

Sole, Richard V., and Brian Goodwin. *Signs of Life: How Complexity Pervades Biology*. New York: Basic Books, 2000.

Strobel, Lee. *The Case for a Creator*. Grand Rapids: Zondervan, 2004.

———. *The Case for Christ*. Grand Rapids: Zondervan, 1998.

Templeton, John Marks, ed. *Evidence of Purpose*. New York: Continuum, 1994.

Tenney, Merrill C., and Steven Barabas, eds. *The Zondervan Pictorial Encyclopedia of the Bible*. 5 vols. Grand Rapids: Zondervan, 1976.

Torrey, Joseph, and D.D. Burlington. "Essay on Inspiration." *Bibliotheca Sacra* 15 (1858) 314–46.

Unger, Merrill F. *Archaeology and the Old Testament*. Grand Rapids: Zondervan, 1954.

Walvoord, John F. *Daniel: The Key to Prophetic Revelation*. Chicago: Moody Press, 1971.

———, and Roy B. Zuck. *The Bible Knowledge Commentary*. 2 vols. Wheaton: Victor Books, 1986.

Whedon, D.A. "Greek Text of the New Testament." *Methodist Quarterly Review* 9 (July 1868) 325–46.

Whiston, William, trans. *The Works of Josephus*. Peabody, MA: Hendrickson, 1987.

Whitaker, William. *A Disputation on Holy Scripture*. Cambridge: Cambridge University Press, 1849.

Wiseman, Donald J. "Archaeological Confirmation of the Old Testament." In *Revelation and the Bible*, edited by Carl Henry. Grand Rapids: Baker, 1958.

Wright, G. Frederick. "Dr. Brigg's 'Wither.'" *Bibliotheca Sacra* 47 (1890) 136–53.

Woods, Leonard. *Lectures on the Inspiration of the Scriptures*. Andover: Flagg and Gould, 1829.

Yamauchi, Edwin. "The Corroborating Evidence." In *The Case for Christ*, by Lee Strobel. Grand Rapids: Zondervan, 1998.